THE JEWISH FAMILY
A Survey and Annotated Bibliography

BENJAMIN SCHLESINGER
Editorial Consultant Florence Strakhovsky

The Jewish Family

A SURVEY AND ANNOTATED BIBLIOGRAPHY

University of Toronto Press

Printed in Canada

ISBN 0-8020-1749-5

Two are better than one.

ECCLESIASTES 4:9

Whosoever spends his days without a wife

Has no joy, nor blessing, or good in his life.

TALMUD - YEVAMOT 62B

Before a man marries, his love goes to his parents;

after he marries, his love goes to his wife.

MIDRASH, PIRKE DE RABBI ELIEZER 32

When you are twenty years of age 'build thy house.'

Marry a wife of good family, beautiful in form and character.

Pay no regard to money, for true wealth consists of

a sufficiency of bread to eat and raiment to wear.

JOSEPH IBN CASPI, 1297-1340

An old maid who gets married becomes a young wife.

JEWISH FOLK PROVERB

Contributors

Jack Balswick is Assistant Professor, Department of Sociology, University of Georgia.

Israel Ellman is Lecturer on Contemporary Jewry, Hashomer Hatzair Study Centre, Givat Haviva, Israel, and a member of Kibbutz Yasur.

Benjamin Schlesinger is Professor, School of Social Work, University of Toronto, and the author of *The Multi-Problem Family: A Review and Annotated Bibliography* (1963), *Poverty in Canada and the United States: Overview and Annotated Bibliography* (1966), and *The One-Parent Family: Perspectives and Annotated Bibliography* (1969).

Florence Strakhovsky, editorial consultant for this volume, is Research Secretary, Centre for Research in the Social and Health Services, University of Toronto.

Contents

APPENDIXES

Preface

Through the centuries, the family has always occupied the central place in Judaism as the primary socio-religious unit. Of all the historical and sociological reasons attributed to Jewish survival, it has been the Jewish concept of family life that has been the major factor. Now, in an open and changing society, the problems facing the family are legion. As Norman Linzer has noted in *The Jewish Family,* the processes of social and technological change have contributed to obsolescence of traditional values, secularization of religion, role diffusion, identity crises, generation gaps in terms of youth's lack of communication and identification with parents, and compartmentalization of family responsibilities and their allocation to surrogate institutions. Jewish families today are not as closely knit as in the past, have less authority over family members, serve ineffectively as role models and protective socialization units, and have also experienced social pathology and breakdown of values as a result of their acculturation to the larger society.

Work on the present book was started two years ago, when I was asked to give an Adult Education course on the Jewish family at Holy Blossom Temple in Toronto. In my first search for source material in English I found very little available, especially socio-psychological studies of modern Jewish family life. That same year I was chairman of a workshop at the Groves Conference on the Family in Boston on the topic of Intermarriage, where professionals who had done studies in this area gathered to share recent information. With the help of a grant from the Memorial Foundation of Jewish Culture I began to gather bibliographical items related to the Jewish family. During my visit to Israel in the summer of 1969 I contacted the Librarian at the Hebrew University in Jerusalem, who kindly sent me copies of all their relevant catalogue cards. Last year a Humanities and Social Science Research grant from the University of Toronto enabled me to visit major libraries in New York City, Montreal, Ottawa, Toronto, and Cleveland which contained sizeable Judaic collections. The grant also helped with costs involved in the production of this volume.

The objective of the annotated bibliography, which contains 429 items, was to select from published materials items in English on Jewish family life. Four essays were chosen for inclusion in the first part of the book to emphasize some significant developments related to Jewish family life. The first is a condensed review by me of family life from biblical times to the shtetl of Eastern Europe. The second essay by Jack Balswick asks the question "Are American Jewish families closely knit?" The third paper by Israel Ellman reviews existing studies of intermarriage among Jews in the United States; and the last essay, by me, examines family life in the kibbutz of Israel, a new Jewish family pattern. Permission to reprint the Balswick and Ellman articles was graciously given by the authors and publishers (*Jewish Social Studies* and *Dispersion and Unity*).

The Appendix contains a list of 172 books which deal with Jewish life in fiction, and statistical tables which cover the world Jewish population of 1968, as well as the addresses of the publishers of the entries listed in the annotated bibliography.

I am grateful to the two sources mentioned for their financial help; to Dr. Albert Rose, Director of the School of Social Work, for permission to complete the manuscript during the summer of 1970; to Florence Strakhovsky for her continued editorial help in the final preparation of the text; and to Helen Romanick, who prepared the manuscript for offset reproduction. Other people who were involved in the production of this book were Dorothy Jenkins, Rachel Schlesinger, and Sadie Gerridzen - to all of them grateful thanks.

B. Schlesinger

PART 1

A Survey

BENJAMIN SCHLESINGER

The Jewish family in retrospect

THE FAMILY IN THE BIBLE[1]

The "woman of valor" at the end of the Book of Proverbs illustrates the full program of the biblical woman's life. She had charge of the preparation and distribution of food in the household; she directed the household arts and was chief steward. She was the business manager, but so far as field work was concerned she confined her activities to garden and vineyard, and apparently left the ploughing and threshing and gleaning to the men. She directed the labor of the female slaves and had in her charge the distribution of charity, an essential part of the duties of an honorable family. Undoubtedly a great deal was expected of her, but her freedom seems to have far exceeded that of women in other ancient cultures. The Book of Proverbs itself shows that her family treated her with deference. There is no instance in the Bible of brutal treatment of a wife by a husband, and women appear as prophetesses, as queens, as poets, and as wise persons whose counsel would prevail in war.

But all of this is far from indicating any equality between man and woman in biblical times. The family type was definitely patriarchal, with a decided male dominance. The inferior status of the wife was distinct. Her adultery was punishable with death. Her husband was her master; she addressed him as "my lord," (*ba'al*). There is no evidence that she had control of any property, except as her husband's agent. He might divorce her at will by a simple "bill of divorcement." To be sure, there were certain restrictions upon divorce, but not many, and she could not under any circumstances divorce her husband.

There is no reliable evidence that a state of promiscuity existed between the sexes in classical Hebrew history. Chastity of women was at all times carefully guarded. Even the early practice of having religious devotees at shrines was summarily condemned. Circumcision seems to have been a rite at first connected with marriage, only later put at birth as a token of tribal relationship and religious acceptability to the national deity.

The normal and usual form of marriage was by purchase. It was a patriarchal process wherein the wife was taken into the family group of the husband, who set up independently of his father when he became full grown. The bride's father provided a dowry, and he and her brothers continued to keep vigilance over her welfare. Marriage seemed to involve little or no rite or ceremony, usually being arranged by the elders of the contracting couple, but the bride's consent was sought. A feast, sometimes lasting many days, marked the wedding proper, part of which must have been the chanting of love lyrics such as those remaining in the Song of Songs. In Israel, the husband had merely the administration of the dowry, which, at the dissolution of the marriage by death or divorce, went back to its source.

In addition to the marriage portion or dowry, there was a marriage price called the *mohar* which the groom's family was obliged to pay - usually to the father of the girl. It was also possible to earn a wife by services, as Jacob served seven years each for Leah and Rachel. Intermarriage with people other than Hebrews was a common practice at all periods. After the settlement in Canaan, when non-Hebrew wives worshipped gods other than the national deity, there was growing opposition to such unions.

Children were well cared for in the Hebrew household. Filial devotion was the foundation virtue of the home, shared equally by father and mother - as instructed in the Fifth Commandment. Undutiful conduct was more than a moral offence; it was a capital crime. On the other hand, all children were considered precious and it was the duty of parents to have as many offspring as possible. While there were no formal schools in biblical times, teaching of children was a parental obligation, largely in religious and ethical matters.

In inheritance of property, primogeniture seems to have been the rule, in the earlier days the first born receiving practically all, while later several sons might divide the estate, the eldest receiving a double portion. This system did not involve an absolute grant of power rights, through which fact alone the system seemed to tend toward a humane way of settling inheritance. Furthermore, a widow, daughter, or even a slave might inherit property.

Divorce was possible for the husband, and though the woman had certain protection the process was simply a matter of record. Widows and orphans became the wards of the people as a whole, and a man's character was tested by his conduct toward these helpless members of the community. Human sacrifice was already taboo in the days of the Bible. It might be noted in passing that the biblical family included with the husband, wife, and children, slaves and "strangers within the gates" who were to be treated with all respect due to human beings and who came within all laws that appertained to the basic family itself.

Evidence would point to the fact that the family more than the individual was the unit of ancient society. Brav states:

The function of the family, then, in ancient Israel, was to propogate the species, to satisfy human needs, to perpetuate religious life – in short, to serve as the fundamental unit of the social order. In its most primitive form, the family determined right and wrong, made laws, administered justice and maintained divine worship, and these characteristics tended to adhere for a long period. The father's authority over the child was almost absolute, and was but rarely abused. Strong family solidarity was a matter of course.[2]

THE TALMUDIC PERIOD

In the first centuries of the Christian era, marriage was regarded not only as the normal state, but as a divine ordinance. Celibacy was uncommon and was definitely disapproved. A man had to be able to support a wife before taking one, but early marriages were favored for sound moral and social reasons. The institution of marriage had for its object the begetting of children, the motive expressed in the law. For girls there were no independent careers to compete with motherhood, and to remain unmarried or to have no offspring was a "bitter misfortune."

Marriages were usually arranged by the parents of the parties. Betrothal was a formal act by which the woman became legally the man's wife. The term used for betrothal, *kiddushin* (sanctification), has religious associations; it was an act by which the woman was consecrated to her husband, "set apart for him exclusively." Unfaithfulness on her part was adultery and punishable as such. Some time elapsed after the formal agreement – which might have been made while both or either contracting parties were minors – before the bride was taken to her husband's house and the marriage consummated. Twelve months is stated as the normal interval in the case of a maiden, much less in the case of a widow.

While divorce was disapproved by many authorities and various restraints put upon it, it was legitimate on certain grounds such as suspected unchastity, proved adultery, or barrenness after ten years of marriage, though the grounds need not have been too specific, so liberal was the general interpretation of the law. A woman could not divorce her husband, but she could sue for divorce in the courts, which might require the husband to give her a bill of divorce, a *get*, for such causes as impotence, denial of conjugal rights, unreasonable restrictions of her freedom of movement, or loathsome ailments. Yet, for all its permissibility, divorce seems to have been quite infrequent.

The woman's place was in the home, that of her father till she was married, then that of her husband as wife, mother, and housekeeper. But the husband was bound by the marriage contract to work for his wife's support, and provide for her food, clothing, and other needs. Her duties included grinding meal, baking, washing clothes, cooking, nursing her child, working in wool, and keeping the house in order. On the other hand, she was constantly protected by the law in that her husband might have only the income and never the principal of his wife's dowry, which in the event of her divorce went with her.

A new feature that entered into the marriage ceremony was the drawing up of a marriage contract - *ketubah* - which had been unknown in biblical times. This legal document, handed to the bride at the marriage ceremony, guaranteed her protection in the event of the husband's death or of her being divorced. In fact, this contract was one of the agencies instituted for the purpose of making divorce more difficult and thus only a last resort.

Four basic Jewish family values have been developed through the Talmud and have governed the Jewish family for many centuries.[3] The first is referred to as *taharath mishpacha* (purity of the family) and is founded on a sane, wholesome appraisal of the sexual relationship in human affairs. Sex is seen as a force for good in life, a gift of God to be cherished, guided, and used only under the guidance of love to fulfil divine purposes in life: namely, to propogate the human race, to perpetuate the Jewish people and thereby the teachings for which Israel continues its mission among the nations, to strengthen and deepen the companionship of husband and wife, and to promote their physical and psychological well-being. This involves chastity prior to marriage and absolute fidelity within the marriage bond. The sexual act cannot be dissociated from the totality of human experience, thus distorting its importance for human happiness. The procreative function of the individual is correlated with a responsibility he or she has to the well-being of the group. The full equality of women in family matters is assumed. All double standards of morality are excluded, and the home must be responsible for the sound sex education of oncoming generations.

Beyond family purity, a second Jewish value is *gidul uboneth* (the obligation for effective child-bearing and child-rearing). An imperative of Jewish living is scrupulous care for the physical, social, educational, and religious needs of the child. This is a central parental responsibility; other people or agencies only assist. Parents are always the child's most impressive teachers, and are obligated to set an example for him by word and conduct, by inter-personal relationships, by participation in community service, and by the full practice of Judaism at home and abroad. Every facet of the child's education is a parental concern and demands close attention, not the least important being the child's moral and religious training. For the child is the living vehicle for the transmission and fulfilment of the entire socio-religious culture of the Jewish people. He is the guarantee of the continuity and progressive creative evolution of that culture towards its highest goals.

A third value can be called *kibud av vo-em*, or filial responsibility. The child is not only the object of affectionate care by parents, who are God's trustees in this relationship; the child has concomitant obligations, particularly the duty to honor and respect his father and mother as long as they live - indeed, as long as the child lives. It is presumed that parents will be so faithful to the trust of their office that they will deserve and win those reactions to their authority that bring lasting satisfactions. But for the child, there is an ongoing challenge to reflect credit and honor upon his parents, to provide them with a status of distinction and dignity, even in their old age, and to perpetuate their memory after death.

The fourth value of family life is *shalom bayith*, or family compatibility. On one hand, the home is intended to give each individual in it the opportunity for the fullest development and expression of his personality so that the greatest measure of personal happiness may be achieved. On the other hand, there is a group happiness of equal importance to be considered - a sense of community, solidarity, and unity, of which all family members constantly must be mindful, and upon the attainment of which their finest qualities of heart and mind and spirit need to be concentrated. *Shalom bayith* is the peace of mind commonly experienced and enjoyed when each individual is contributing his full share to the feeling of the wholeness of the household, the effecting of a salutary total family personality. On the negative side, when husband and wife cannot work together harmoniously to this end, and efforts at reconciliation have failed, Judaism classically provided for divorce and allows for it as a last resort. On the positive side, however, this value involves (1) coordinating the fulfilment of individual potentialities and aspirations, (2) a strong feeling of identity with others in the close and the larger family groups, (3) a pooling of resources for the benefit of all, and (4) a healthy sense of family pride. This is the domestic expression of Judaism's passion for oneness, in God, in Israel, and in humanity - this oneness of the family.

These values enabled the Jewish people to survive physically as a group despite the ravages of social disease and the ruthless hostility of neighbors. They normalized the sexual relationship by insuring security for all concerned - father, mother, and child; they prevented the sex act from being dissociated from the totality of human experience; and they correlated the procreative function of the individual with the responsibility he or she has for the well-being of his social group.

THE MIDDLE AGES[4]

Monogamy, which for fifteen hundred years had been the almost unfailing Jewish practice, became a legal mandate of Judaism in the Western world around the year 1000 of the Christian era. Bigamy was prohibited on pain of excommunication and divorce without consent of the wife was forbidden. Divorces on the grounds established in Talmudic days were not rare. Marriages were frequently contracted at so early an age that divorce often occurred before the marriage was really consummated. Divorced girls easily remarried, for divorce carried no stigma with it. Divorces among adults who had lived long together were quite exceptional in Jewish life.

The standard Jewish law code, the *Shulchan Aruch*, first printed in 1564, laid down the rule: "It is the duty of every Jewish man to marry a wife in his eighteenth year, but he who anticipates and marries earlier is following the more laudable course; but no one should marry before he is thirteen." Arrangements were in almost all cases left to the parents, though cases of marriage resulting from romantic love are not unknown. Usually a professional match-maker, or *shadchan*, would bring the desirability of a particular couple's mating to the attention of their parents, or would be employed by a parent to seek out a match. These professionals were sometimes supplanted by rabbis in their tasks. Fathers were much more anxious to obtain learned and respectable rather than wealthy sons-in-law.

Naturally, child-marriages were not without serious consequences, as the prevalence of divorce indicates. It is clear that a boy in his teens would be unable to set up a house of his own. Of necessity, the youthful husband often resided in the home of his bride's father or was maintained by the latter for a period more or less definitely fixed beforehand. This was likely to encourage the habit of dependence. It further encouraged the growth of marriage by proxy, a custom common to all mediaeval Europe.

Parent-child relationships remained on the high level of the past. There was little affectionate demonstrativeness, but care and attention on the one hand and devotion and honor on the other were seldom missing. In a way, a child's life was not easy. Discipline was severe and corporal punishment habitual. Behavior at the table, in synagogue, and in the presence of elders generally was strictly regulated. Play was frequent but not regular. Education for boys was almost universal, usually beginning at the age of five and continuing until at least thirteen, with often ten or more hours a day spent in the classroom. Girls received their principal training at home, but occasionally were noted for their learning.

Domesticity in Jewish men, long a noted characteristic, dates from this period. Their knowledge of the minutiae of the home ritual gave them a personal role in the kitchen and in the market place. The wife had a home-loving lord, who perhaps derived some of his devotion to his family from his intimate participation in all the pleasures and anxieties of home management. Considering that the home was the scene of some of the most touching and inspiring religious rites, that the sanctity of the home was an affectionate tradition linking the Jew to his past, that amidst the degradation heaped upon him throughout the Middle Ages he was emancipated at least in one spot on earth, that he learned from his domestic peace to look with pitying rather than vindictive eyes on his persecutors, it becomes obvious what a powerful influence the home wielded in forming and refining Jewish character. Jewish domestic morals in the Middle Ages were beyond reproach.

Heinrich Heine summarized the Jewish family in the Middle Ages when he wrote,

The Jewish home was a haven of rest from the storms that raged round the very gates of the ghettos, nay, a fairy palace in which the bespattered objects of the mob's derision threw off their garb of shame and resumed the royal attire of freemen. The home was the place where the Jew was at his best. In the marketplace he was perhaps hard and sometimes ignoble; in the world he helped his judges to misunderstand him; in the home he was himself.[5]

FAMILY LIFE IN THE SHTETL (SMALL TOWN) OF EASTERN EUROPE[6]

The shtetl life as described here has disappeared, mostly due to the Bolshevik revolution and the Nazi occupation. It cannot be said, in 1970, to represent a living organism, but only a glimpse into the past. Immigrants who landed on North American shores brought this type of life with them, but it quickly faded under the impact of the influences to which it was subjected in the new land. Many writers nostalgically recall their youth and describe, for example, life on the East Side of New York as approximating the shtetl community.

For its inhabitants the shtetl was less the physical town than the people who lived in it. "My shtetl" meant "my community," and community meant the Jewish community. Traditionally, the human rather than the physical environment had always been given primary importance. Emphasis on the Jewish community was inevitable, for historical developments had excluded it from membership in the larger community. Socially and legally it was an entity in itself, subject to special laws and responsible, within strict limits, for regulating and conducting itself.

The shtetl grew up in the ghetto atmosphere which had been created by the European nations from the fourteenth century onwards. The ghetto was an area within a city which was reserved for residence of Jews and to which Jews were confined by law. Jews developed their own social, political, and economic life. Their religious life revolved around the synagogue. The real inner solidarity of the ghetto community always lay in its strong family ties. In this inner circle deep bonds of sympathy had been woven among the members through colorful ritual. Here each individual, a mere Jew to the world outside, had a place of dignity and was bound to the rest by profound sentiments. Through the organization of the synagogue, in turn, the family unit was given a definite status, based not so much on wealth as on learning, piety, purity of family life, and services rendered to the community.

The shtetl mother had many roles to play in the family. She was the wife, who ordered the functioning of the household, and the mother, the key figure in the family constellation. Often she was the breadwinner if her husband fulfilled the ideal picture of the man as a scholar. She managed the fiscal affairs of the home, was the chief counselor, and shopped, cleaned the house, ran a business, or kept a stall at the market. The woman of the house, in other words, was the mother of the whole family, including the father. When she offered food, she was offering her love and she offered it constantly. When her food was refused it was as if her love were rejected. She had to conduct a "Yiddish" home, "keep kosher," and observe the many religious observances around the household. The typical love that has been attributed to the *mamme* (mother) was that of "mother will love you always no matter what happens." She may have had odd ways of showing it but the belief in mother's love was strong and unshakeable.

The mother's love was manifested in two ways, by constant and solicitous overfeeding and by unremitting concern about every aspect of her child's welfare, expressed for the most part in unceasing verbalization. "What have you done? What are you going to do? Are you warm enough? Put on another muffler. Have you had enough to eat? Look, take just a little of this soup."

Inherent in this maternal love was the idea of boundless suffering and sacrifice. Parents "killed" themselves for their children. Children were reminded constantly of this suffering on their behalf. The ideal shtetl mother, toiling constantly for her family, was an eternal fountain of sacrifice, lamentation, and renewed effort. Mother love was also expressed in "worry." If one worried actively enough, something might come of it: "You worry yourself out." The intensity of one's worry showed the extent of identification, another proof of love.

Both parents were entitled to *derekh erets* (respect). The mother was celebrated in folk songs as "my love for her," "for me," "her constancy," "her sacrifice," "there were no other mothers like her." The mother's suffering became also a weapon, as a control for the future. This was the point at which the mother expected the debts to be paid by the children. She was saying, "I have suffered for you, now behave, and do what I say so that I should not suffer more" – a very good control, with overt verbal expressions. The shining reward that the mother was to receive was that her children should *shepn naches* (gather joys).

In return for the "sacrifices" of the mother, the child was obligated to support his old mother. A mother would refuse help from her children as long as possible, feeling that her role was to give and not to receive. But if necessity forced her, she would accept, and use this as a boast, "They do everything for me; they watch me like an eye in the head." Sons and daughters who worked gave their wages to the mother, as did the father. Even when the children were carrying most of the economic burden, the parents still felt that they themselves were supporting the family. "Isn't it their home?" One's own children were "my own flesh and blood."

The realm of the father (*tatte*) was the spiritual and intellectual. He had the official authority, the final word about matters of the moment. However, he might be advised, coached, or opposed in private by the mother. "When he talked everybody was quiet, and when he slept no one made any noise." The father, in contrast to the father in the Middle Ages, was a more remote figure, psychologically and often literally, than the mother. He might be away from home a great deal. "Children, and household, are not a man's business." He might spend much time studying in the synagogue, or he might be a traveling merchant.

The father enjoyed tremendous respect, from the very small members of the family to the married sons. "You should see him when he comes home from the synagogue. All his children are around him; they help him to take off his coat; he does not speak to them; he sits down at the table. Often he closes his eyes and meditates." Or, "Sometimes a child is noisy, so the father looks at the child from under his eyebrows, and that is enough. He does not have to speak to the child; he only looks."

This respect was not rooted in fear. "A look is not a threat; it is only a reminder to behave." The respect for the father extended to his possessions when he was not present. His chair, his shoes, were all part of him. The father administered punishment, chiefly for some infraction of the moral or social code. Any criticism of him would constitute disrespect. "He knows what he does." The father then was a kind of respected figure who did not take part in the household routine, but devoted his time to learning or business. Thus the mother was left in full control of the children and the household.

The mother had only a little time to really get to know her son; at the early age of four he started to go to the *cheder* (school), and she had less influence over him. Thus the fixation of the mother-child relation was on the earliest infantile level. The time when she could love him, and care for him, was when he was a baby, before the world of men claimed him. There was a pride in being a mother, and this brought with it feelings of accomplishment.

The Eastern European mother saw her child, at any age, as a terribly vulnerable baby, incapable of taking care of himself, who would perish without her constant vigilance. At the same time, the baby appeared as terribly strong. The mother was a righteous figure, capable of damning or giving absolution. She was a suffering person, being incessantly wounded, and deriving a satisfaction and unacknowledged emotional gratification in this masochistic way.

It would be folly to suggest that maternal overprotection is a uniquely Jewish phenomenon. If one compares the Jewish mother with Philip Wylie's "Mom," who uses overprotection as a simple strategem to keep her children, especially her sons, in a state of sulky submission, and whose need to dominate is little more than the urge to maintain her spoiled status, one sees a definite difference. With the Eastern European mother the situation was at once more complex and more tragic. She was overprotective, but there was real anxiety present. In Jewish overprotection we see the results of the rearing of children in an atmosphere of fear and anxiety, a defensive gesture against the imminence of trauma.

From overfeeding to "sacrifice" the shtetl mother clung to the children. Using analytical concepts, the overprotection can be seen as an expression of and compensation for unconscious hostility and rejection. The mother, unable to face her own hostile feelings, swaddles these same feelings in excessive solicitude for her child. And yet this seems too slick, in the light of Jewish experience, to be accepted as it stands.

Most explanations for Jewish overprotectiveness can be found in Jewish cultural patterns and in the Jewish past. Overprotection can be seen as a reflex against a long, harrowing history of persecution. In the ghetto, where there was an ever-present fear of danger, the wife became the family power and authority; thus there seemed to be a transposition of roles. The scholarly husband became subtly feminized, the bulwark mother took on a masculine tone. She ran the family. The price one paid for family cohesiveness and intensity was dependence. Thus we can understand the anguish with which a child would leave home. The emphasis on the learning of the boy, and the anxiety that parents felt towards their children's education, may be similar to the feeling of "seizing the future by the throat." Obviously, if so much was at stake in a child, he must be cherished and encouraged and protected. We tend to repeat the pattern, we rebel against it most passionately, and the Jewish girl may rage against the overprotective mother. To be sure, it is now sanctified with the books and theories of modern psychology, but what we may very well get is "the iron fist in a mental hygiene glove."

Yet much of what has been created by Jewish people all over the world has come from the families in which this pattern of overprotectiveness had been in operation for generations. One explanation may be that "Jews tend to be overprotective because for so long they have been underprotected."

Any nostalgia for the security of the past should not blind us to the well-known weaknesses of traditional East European Jewish family life, particularly as it lacked opportunity to adjust to modern life, not only because of isolation in the ghetto but also because of its own authoritarian orthodoxy which handicapped adjustment. We also know that every shtetl had at least one local village *meshugenar* (fool) so there was no absence of neuroses in that family structure.

However, not overlooking its weaknesses, the East European Jewish attitude toward the family was on the whole realistic as well as sanctified, and its stability was related to a strong sense of obligation to the survival of the Jewish group. This culture of the shtetl no longer exists. It remains to be seen just how long even some of the mood of this passing Jewish family tradition will survive the modern tempo, though one would like to believe these words of Margaret Mead in her preface to the study of the shtetl: "with the traditional capacity of the Jews to preserve the past, while transmuting it into a healthy relationship to the present, much of the faith and hope which lived in the shtetl will inform the lives of the descendants of the shtetl in other lands."[7]

One of the best summaries of classical Jewish family life was given by Nahum N. Glatzer, professor of Jewish history at Brandeis University, when he addressed the one hundredth anniversary dinner of the Jewish Family and Community Service in Chicago on September 20, 1959.[8] His five points were:

First, the Jewish family was a patriarchal family. The father and, at his side, the mother were authorities, not pals and playmates. The younger and the older generations communicated, but the distinction between them remained and was strongly maintained. Parents were never addressed by their names; they were always "father" and "mother." This set them apart from the generation of children. The gulf was bridged by love, an attitude of loving concern. The tension between the generations - which often led, as it does, to friction - was intended to be a creative tension. It implied the existence of standards of life and of action; the natural anarchy in the child's mind found its corrective in the standards of right and wrong, of what was good and what was evil, that the parent was supposed to represent.

Second, the Jewish family was, as a rule, a three-generation family. Grandparents were an integral part of the group. Far from being a nuisance, a burden, and removed from the realities of day-to-day living, they had an irreplaceable contribution to make. In a practically unchanging world, their wise counsel, based on long experience, was valuable. And beyond this, they symbolized continuity of life, a measure of timelessness; this gave them an almost sacred quality.

Third, the Jewish home fostered the wholeness of life. A home was the stage on which the drama of life unfolded. Home life consisted of birth and education, common reading and common singing, sickness and recovery, family celebrations, and , yes, family quarrels, courtship, marriage, and the serenity of old age. Add to these the simple, prosaic, material pursuits that supplemented the emotional and intellectual aspects of life.

Fourth, into the framework of the individual Jewish family life was fitted the colorful picture of Israel's sancta: the Sabbaths and holidays, feasts and fasts, each one of them recalling an event of the past in which the child participated. There was the exodus from Egypt after long bondage; the wandering in the desert with its saints and its rebels; the victory of the Maccabeans over the tyrant Antiochus; the tragedy of Jerusalem's fall; and the promise of redemption. Year after year, the child, in celebrating the Sabbaths, relived the thrill of creation of light out of darkness; of the dawn of humanity on its cumbersome way towards knowledge of itself, the world, and its Maker; of the rise and fall of generations; of the drama of Israel, searching for a life of nobility and peace in a world of war and violence.

Fifth, the Jewish family was a learning family. The ideal father took time out from his business or his craft to immerse himself in the study of the sacred books, the Bible and its commentaries, Talmud or Midrash. He did this either in the privacy of his home or by joining a study group in his synagogue. His mind was trained to concentrate on specific problems, as a rule problems of law. He was taught to respect differences of opinion, to search for a level of honest agreement. Not the gathering of useful information was the goal, but the open and receptive mind, the striving for a rational order in a world imperiled by forces of chaos. The ideal son, therefore, prepared himself for entry into this world of books, ideas, and learning, a world in which the great disgrace was to be called an ignoramus.

The pursuit of learning was meant to be perennial.

To sum up, the Jewish family stood for *standards* of life and action; it strove for continuity; it considered itself an integral part of a greater whole; it was an active group, with the home as its center; it was a learning group. Under ideal circumstances this type of family could counteract fragmentation of life; it could achieve a measure of wholeness.

NOTES

1 I am indebted to the work of Stanley Brav for the major trends in the biblical family discussed here. *Marriage and the Jewish Tradition,* ed. Stanley R. Brav (New York, 1951).
2 *Marriage and the Jewish Tradition,* p. 88.
3 For a full discussion of these values see Leon S. Lang, "Jewish Values in Family Relationships," *Conservative Judaism,* I (June 1945), 9-18.
4 For a complete picture of Jewish family life in the Middle Ages see Israel Abrahams, *Jewish Life in the Middle Ages* (New York, 1958).
5 *Ibid.,* p. 113.
6 For a complete discussion of life in the shtetl see M. Zborowski, and E. Herzog, *Life Is with People* (New York, 1955).
7 *Zborowski and Herzog,* p. 19.
8 See Nahum N. Glatzer, "The Jewish Family and Humanistic Values," *Journal of Jewish Communal Service,* XXXVI (Spring 1969), 269-273.

JACK BALSWICK

Are American Jewish families closely knit?

A review of the literature

This paper tries to answer the question, "are Jewish families closely knit?" An attempt was made to utilize writings and research material of the last twenty years. Information was sought wherever it could be obtained: in books dealing with the family, with religion, with the Jew, and in numerous journals and periodicals. An inclusive search of the issues of the last twenty years was made of a number of relevant journals and periodicals.[1]

My overall preliminary impression is that there has been very little empirical research dealing with the question of closeness of the American Jewish family. As a result, much of the material presented will be both historical and impressionistic. The empirical data, along with the more subjective data, will be used together in an attempt to arrive at an idea of the closeness of the Jewish family. It should be emphasized that any conclusions drawn in this paper are highly tentative and subject to further investigation.

THE JEWISH FAMILY

The Jewish family, as Gordon has it, was traditionally regarded as a "miniature sanctuary" since spiritual and moral qualities of God were taught directly and by example in the home. The father as the head of the family had the responsibility of rearing his children in the fear of God and the knowledge of His law. Like the patriarch of the Hebrew Bible, he was the towering personality who protected and disciplined the members of his household. As his helpmate, his wife was the teacher and moral guide of the family. Her duties and responsibilities were domestic - associated with the home. She was the matriarch who, in submission to her husband, still had much influence and authority. The children were to be obedient and loving toward their parents.[2]

Strodtbeck describes the historic Jewish family, particularly as it was found in Europe before it came to America, as follows: "The Jewish family was traditionally a close-knit one, but it was the entire Jewish *shtetl* (community) rather than the family which was considered the inclusive social unit and world. Although relatives were more important than friends, all Jews were considered to be bound to each other. ... The primary unit was the family of procreation."[3] Here we find Strodtbeck emphasizing not only the closeness of the Jewish family but also the closeness of the entire Jewish community.

Glasner states that in the Jewish religious culture "the *home* is regarded as the basic religious institution, in which an individual is taught that he can find completion of his personality growth and highest personal fulfilment only in marriage and the continuation of the larger family." These types of attitudes "add to the prepotency of the family's influence and make for greater personal-social stability."[4] Glasner goes on to suggest that "in Judaism one finds that the *central* religious institution has always been the home, not the synagogue." "This goes back to earliest biblical times, when the home-altar was virtually all that was known to our nomadic, pastoral ancestors."

In Judaism there are numerous ceremonies: traditional observances of the Sabbath and various other religious holidays which serve to bring the extended family together frequently, thereby strengthening the influence of the family. Such rites as the circumcision; the *Ben Zakhar* (a special party celebrating the birth of a male child); the *Pidyon ha-Ben* (redemption of the first-born) - all are associated with the "fathering of the clan."[5] Similarly, when death comes to any member of the family, the entire extended family takes part in the mourning and follows the certain ritual patterns involved. Glasner concludes that "such religious family gatherings ... become a highly meaningful and cherished part of the individual family member's psyche."[6]

RESEARCH FINDINGS

Perhaps the best study relating to the question of the cohesiveness of the Jewish family is one by Landis. In this study Landis obtained a sample of three thousand college students in family sociology courses at various colleges in the United States. In analyzing his data he used inductive statistics to verify his findings and found that approximately 80 percent of the Jewish students, 70 percent of the Protestants, 70 percent of the Catholics, and 47 percent of the students with no religious preference reported their parents to be "happy" or "very happy." He also found that the percentages of divorced and separated parents were: Jewish, 3.3; Catholics, 7.7; Protestants, 10; and people of no religious faith, 18.2.[7] These two findings by Landis support the indication that the Jewish family is closely knit when compared with non-Jewish families.

Combining these findings with the previous subjective reasonings of Gordon, Strodtbeck, and Glasner we may be inclined to attribute cohesion within the

Jewish family to Judaism as a religion. However, Landis found that this is not necessarily the case. He found that among the Jewish families there is little relationship between religiousness and parents' marital happiness, while among the other groups there was a positive relationship between religiousness and parents' marital happiness.[8] Landis does not specify by what criteria he assesses degree of religiousness. Should his assessment be faulty, the relationship between family closeness and religiousness could still hold. Be this as it may, since Landis provides us with the more objective facts, we can conclude that although the Jewish family does seem to be closely knit, this does not appear to be a result of high religiousness on their part. It should be kept in mind that Jewish culture includes more than just religion alone.

In degree of closeness to their parents, the Jewish students ranked first and were then followed by Catholic students, Protestant students, and finally by students with no religious faith. A further finding by Landis was that parents of Jewish and Protestant children more than parents of Catholic and non-faith children had given sex information to their children. Also, the Jewish and Protestant children reported less undesirable attitudes and more desirable attitudes towards sex.[9] This set of findings suggests that the Jewish family may not only be more closely knit than non-Jewish families, but, with the exception of the Protestant family, may provide more inter-communication and discussion between family members on the topic of sex. If a family is free in discussing a topic such as sex (which is often avoided as a topic in the American family), we may suppose that they are equally as free in discussing other less "hush-hush" topics. From this, it would be easy to complete this following plausible theory. The more inter-communication between family members, the more positive interaction between family members. The more positive interaction between family members, the more closely knit is the family. Thus, the more inter-communication between family members, the more closely knit is the family. Since the Jewish family has more inter-communication, it is a more closely knit family.

Landis found that, of the four groups, Jews were the least willing to marry outside their faith; with Jewish females being less willing to do so than Jewish males. However, while 41 percent of the Jewish males said they were willing to marry outside their faith, only 13 percent said they were willing to change their faith.[10] This is a further indication of closeness of the Jewish family.

In their book, *Husbands and Wives*, Blood and Wolfe describe the results of a cross-section sample of the entire community of Detroit plus data from a representative sample of farm families. They found that, as long as their income was high, Jewish families were as satisfied with their standard of living as anyone; but, when their income was low, the Jewish family was more dissatisfied with their standard of living than non-Jews with the same income.[11] From this, we might venture to suggest that the Jewish family may be more closely knit among the higher-income families than among the lower-income families. In doing this we are assuming that satisfaction with standard of living is related to family happiness; and family happiness is, in turn, related to the unitedness of the family.

Lenski in *The Religious Factor* presents the results of a part of the Detroit Area Studies of 1952 and 1958. This is a research-training facility of the University of Michigan which conducts a yearly cross-sectional study of the entire community of Detroit. In it are contained some insights on the American Jewish family. In considering the data which will be presented, it must be pointed out that: (1) the Jewish sample contains only twenty-six respondents, and (2) relationships are supported only by descriptive statistics (usually in percentages).

Lenski found that Jews, more than any religious group, were likely to have extended relatives living in Detroit. In this sense, 20 percent of the white Protestants, 10 percent of the Catholics and Negro Protestants, and only 6 percent of the Jews had severed their ties with their extended kin group. This difference between Jews and other religious groups in regard to separation from their kin group was especially pronounced among persons of the middle class. Of this group, 29 percent of the white Protestants, 9 percent of the middle-class Catholics, and none of the middle-class Jews reported "no relatives" living in their community.[12]

The percentage of respondents who visited their relatives every week was as follows: Jews, 75; white Catholics, 56; white Protestants, 49; and Negro Protestants, 46.[13] Here we see that Jews were more likely to visit relatives every week than any other socio-religious group. Lenski also found that Jews, more than any of the other socio-religious groups, felt that husband, wife, children, and parents had the greatest influence on their religious beliefs. These two findings seem to support the proposition that the Jewish family is closely knit, but the finding shown in the following table is in the opposite direction. This table shows (in percentages) answers to the question "whose political opinions had the greatest influence on how you voted?"[14]

	Close friends	Relatives
Jews	50	50
White Protestant	30	70
White Catholic	22	78
Negro Protestant	22	78

If degree of family influence on one's political opinions can be used as an indicator of family closeness, this finding does not support the proposition of the Jewish family being closely knit.

A final relevant finding by Lenski concerns divorce rates. He found that only 4 percent of the Jewish respondents who had ever married reported a divorce, compared with 8 percent of the white Catholics, 16 percent of the white Protestants, and 22 percent of the Negro Protestants.[15] In general, Lenski's study tends to indicate that the Jewish family is more closely knit than the other three socio-religious groups considered.

Strodtbeck compared the Southern Italian and the Jew in New Haven. He reasoned that these two ethnic groups were comparable since, in regard to their arrival from Europe, they were in the same period of residence in New Haven. In this sample a questionnaire was administered to over three thousand boys and girls in the New Haven public and parochial schools. Data obtained were used primarily to identify a set of third-generation Italian and Jewish children.

The findings of this study by Strodtbeck are numerous and with varying degrees of applicability; and thus they are freely summarized in this paper. Strodtbeck found that the Jew, as compared with the Italian, was

1. less likely to say that, "even after marriage a young person's first loyalty is to his parents and that he should not move away from his parents";
2. not different in the amount of time spent in caretaking and in affectionate interaction with the child, the warmth of the mother-child relationship, and the amount of enjoyment in child care;
3. less severe in toilet training;
4. more permissive when it came to sex play on the part of children, masturbation, or nudity in the home;
5. more permissive of children's aggression towards parents;
6. less imposing on the child's table manners, conversations with adults, acting as "boy" or "girl," caution around furniture, and freedom of movement from the home;
7. less prone to follow through and demand obedience on the part of the child;
8. somewhat warmer in regard to the emotional atmosphere of parent-child relations;
9. more likely to place higher value on spanking;
10. more willing to leave home in order to "make one's way in life";
11. more prone to value individualistic rather than collective rewards;
12. more prone to have higher educational and occupational expectations for his sons;
13. more likely to show equality of power in the husband-wife relationship;
14. more prone to expect longer school attendance on the part of the children, while being less insistent on the child's doing well in school.[16]

It is impossible to make a summary statement about these fourteen points. It must be pointed out that – in the sample – the Jews are concentrated in the middle class and the Italians in the lower class. Since the Italian-Jewish differences in class level are not controlled in the comparisons, the exact contribution of "class" in contrast with the "Jewish factor" cannot be ascertained. This simply serves to illustrate the importance of considering interrelatedness among the various social institutions of American society. The sociological approach to the family as a social system must also be applied to the family, religion, social class, etc., as units of a larger social system - namely American society. This point is not only made but demonstrated by Williams in *American Society.* As Znaniecki proposes: "Every empirical object is either a system or an element in a system, or both."[17]

Gordon in *Jews in Suburbia* has insightfully written about the modern Jewish family in suburbia. He suggests that

> The family is still the nuclear institution of the Jewish people in suburbia ... I believe that the suburb has strengthened Jewish family life. Even though the parental roles are somewhat different from what they were a generation ago, the home remains the central institution in Jewish life, and the children are the center of attention and concern for their parents. Whatever the present weakness and defects of suburban life, it is my belief that they may be more than counterbalanced by a more closely knit Jewish family life in the suburban home.[18]

Gordon supports the position that the Jewish family is closely knit, but he also suggests that there have been great changes in the modern Jewish family. He feels that equality is the best description of the modern American Jewish family and marriage. The suburban Jewish family is more of a matriarch, with the wife making most of the decisions and assuming most of the household duties. Gordon suggests that she has been made to fill this vacuum created by the father's preoccupancy with his job.[19] However, findings by Blood and Wolfe suggest that the suburban family may not be as "matriarchal" as originally thought. There is an indication that the Jewish suburban family may be a child-centered family. Gordon found that one of the main reasons for the move to suburbs was "for the good of the children."[20] He also found that 61 percent of the suburban respondents and their children visit with their parents and other relatives at least as frequently as they did when all resided near each other in the central city. The majority of those who report that their visits with parents and relatives are now less frequent attribute this reduction to the increased distance between their homes. Nearly all the respondents were at their parents' homes on the traditional Festival Days.[21] As evident in Gordon's data, it would seem that as this Jewish emphasis on the family continues, the Jewish family in suburbia is still closely knit, at least in tradition, with its extended family.

Wessel, taking a rather psychological approach, suggests that, "the Jewish family, relatively more united than the gentile family, seems to increase in cohesion as it offers an oasis of understanding." She goes on to explain that

The existence of ethnic tensions puts upon the parent the responsibility of seeking aid on emotional individualization of children. There is a tendency also to improve and to strengthen the ethnic community so that it will offer healthy milieu for social participation and for the development of personality. In doing so, the Jewish family only bears witness to theories of family life in general which make the family the agency charged with the responsibility of providing opportunity for the healthy and integrated development of its members.[22]

Wessel argues that the Jewish family is closely knit. It should be pointed out, however, that she gives little statistical evidence to support this contention.

At the time of his death in 1947, W. I. Thomas was in the process of writing a book, *Bintl Brief*, about the American Jew. His work was based on a large number of letters written by American Jews. The data which Thomas assimilated were later analyzed by Bressler.[23] According to Bressler, Thomas thought that the key motif expressed in Jewish family patterns was the effort to preserve the solidarity of the family. Such customs as having the entire kin group meet during holidays and for numerous other occasions served as factors in the establishment of family solidarity. Bressler reports the data in the *Bintl Brief*, suggesting strongly that "the individual seems to possess a high degree of emotional involvement, an intense consciousness of solidarity, and a strong awareness of standards of obligation with reference to both his immediate and larger extended family." It further seemed to Thomas that the intimate involvement with the larger kinship group as an anticipated and normal pattern among Jews was related to their historical reliance on large groups in general, as represented by the community at large. In summary, Thomas' data seem to support the proposition that the Jewish family is closely knit. Although Thomas' methodology was subjective rather than objective, he still must be credited with basing his data on something concrete (it could be considered a type of case study approach) and not just impressionistic opinions.

Through the reading of literature and by personal observation Freund has analyzed the change which has taken place in the Jewish family from its East-European existence to the second-generation Jewish family existing in the United States. Although Freund's analysis is admittedly tentative, he does offer some insightful observations. In comparison with the East-European Jewish family, Freund found the second-generation American Jewish family to be

1. more democratic (father less likely to share high status alone);
2. more mobile;
3. likely to emphasize the secular rather than the religious;
4. less likely to participate in Jewish celebrations;
5. smaller in size;
6. less likely to provide recreational, religious, social, and protective functions;

7. less likely to have in-group solidarity;
8. less likely to transmit Jewish culture;
9. more likely to give all children equally high status (rather than sons only);
10. less likely to regard itself as having high status and role in the community;
11. more permissive of the mother gaining a general education and working outside the home;
12. subordinate to the individual (rather than the individual being subordinate to the family);
13. less likely to view the father with fear and respect;
14. less likely to view marriage as a religious duty;
15. more likely to have mates selected by children instead of parents;
16. less likely to place an emphasis on a dowry;
17. less likely to emphasize marrying someone from the same national origin or place of birth;
18. less reluctant to marry outside of the Jewish religion (this is still discouraged however);
19. more likely to practice birth control and discuss sex matters;
20. less likely to require that young people be chaperoned, and more likely to permit premarital kissing and petting;
21. less likely to provide the individual with a "specific way of life" (the family is no longer the only transmitter of norms and values).[24]

It must be emphasized that these points compare the East-European with the second-generation American Jewish family. These findings do not necessarily have a bearing on the difference between the American Jewish family and the American non-Jewish family. We may expect that the same changes recorded above have taken place among the families of all racial and ethnic groups which have been transplanted from Europe to the United States. Freund's data have been used to give an impression of the difference between the "traditional Jewish family" as it was found in Eastern Europe and the second-generation Jewish family as it has been found in the United States. It seems obvious that the change has been from the closely knit European Jewish family to the less closely knit American Jewish family.

SUMMARY

The data presented have ranged all the way from findings based on probability statistics to highly impressionistic opinions. In each case the information has been presented in an effort to evaluate the cohesiveness of the Jewish family. It is not reasonable to give data of such extreme variety equal weighting; in fact, the non-empirical data would not have been included in this paper had it not been for the shortage of both theoretical and empirical material related to the topic. It is not meant to suggest that the more impressionistic ideas have no value, they certainly do - especially in providing possible hypotheses and propositions which can be tested. But if empirical data were on hand, there would be no need for this impressionistic material. Its function would have been exhausted with the formulation of research.

The next obvious question is: where do we stand in regard to our knowledge of the unity of the Jewish family? We can state that

1. some empirical research has been done which can be applied to our topic;
2. this empirical research has *not* been devised to test the specific topic at hand;
3. to my knowledge, there has not previously been any attempt made to scientifically test the proposition that the Jewish family is closely knit.

Since the purpose of this paper is to search the literature dealing with this topic and not an empirical test of it, no definite conclusions can be stated.

CONCLUSION

On the basis of the data used in this paper, it may be stated that the American Jewish family is closely knit. It is more closely knit than non-Jewish families with which it has been compared. The results have not been all-inclusive and the control groups may or may not be representative of American non-Jewish families in general. In conclusion, however, it does appear that the findings of this paper should enable us to proceed towards further research with the hypothesis that *the American Jewish family is closely knit as compared to the American non-Jewish family.*

NOTES

1 These journals and periodicals being the *American Sociological Review, American Journal of Sociology, Marriage and Family Living, Jewish Social Studies,* and *Commentary.*
2 Albert I. Gordon, *Jews in Suburbia* (Boston, 1959), pp. 57-58.
3 Fred L. Strodtbeck, "Family Interaction, Values, and Achievement," in Marshall Sklare, ed., *The Jew* (Glencoe, 1958), p. 151.
4 Samuel Glasner, "Family Religion as a Matrix of Personal Growth," *Marriage and Family Living,* XXII (August 1961), 291.
5 *Ibid.,* 292.
6 *Ibid.,* 292-293.
7 Judson T. Landis, "Religiousness, Family Relationships, and Family Values in Protestant, Catholic, and Jewish Families," *Marriage and Family Living,* XXII (November 1960), 342.

8 *Ibid.*
9 *Ibid.,* 343, 347.
10 *Ibid.,* 345.
11 Robert O. Blood, and Donald M. Wolfe, *Husbands and Wives* (Glencoe 1960), pp. 109-110.
12 Gerhard Lenski, *The Religious Factor* (Garden City, 1961; rev. ed., Anchor Books, 1963), p. 215.
13 *Ibid.,* p. 216.
14 *Ibid.,* p. 217.
15 *Ibid.,* p. 218.
16 Strodtbeck, "Family Interaction, Values, and Achievement," pp. 151-164. These findings are cited by Strodtbeck as coming from B. Tregoe's "An Analysis of Ethnic and Social Class Differences," an unpublished ms based on research materials collected by the staff of the Laboratory of Human Development, Harvard University.
17 Don Martindale, *The Nature and Types of Sociological Theory* (Boston, 1960), p. 468.
18 Gordon, *Jews in Suburbia,* pp. 83-84.
19 *Ibid.,* pp. 59-60.
20 *Ibid.,* p. 74.
21 *Ibid.,* pp. 74-75.
22 Bessie Bloom Wessel, "Ethnic Family Patterns: The American Jewish Family," *American Journal of Sociology,* IV (May 1948), p. 441.
23 Marvin Bressler, "Selected Family Patterns in W. I. Thomas' Unfinished Study of the Bintl Brief," *American Sociological Review,* XVII (1952), 563-571.
24 Michael Freund, "Tentative Analysis of Differences between the Small-Town Jewish Family in Eastern Europe and the First- and Second-Generation Jewish Family in the United States," mimeo. New York, Training Bureau for Jewish Communal Services, 1950, pp. 1-6.

ISRAEL ELLMAN

Jewish intermarriage in the United States of America

INTRODUCTION

Intermarriage is an important indicator in regard to the degree of social integration achieved by the members of a minority group. Milton Gordon[1] sees it as one of the last rungs on the ladder to final integration and assimilation. We believe him to be substantially right.

In the following survey we have attempted to describe the various aspects of intermarriage among Jews today in the United States of America. The didactic and descriptive literature is considerable but we have based ourselves mainly on empirical studies which have been conducted in various parts of the United States. The rate and character of Jewish intermarriage are moulded largely by the given social conditions; these change and with them the whole picture of intermarriage. For that reason we have taken as our basis studies conducted in the 1950s and in the 1960s only. It was not our intention to provide a historical survey, and data taken from studies made thirty to forty years ago may well give a distorted picture of the position as it is today.

DATING PATTERNS OF JEWISH YOUTH

An important indicator for the future incidence of intermarriage is the degree of interreligious dating among students and teen-agers. At the same time, one must take into account the fact that the teen-age and student period is a notoriously unstable one and the patterns prevalent during this period are not necessarily permanent. Caplowitz, Ritterband, and Jarrow of Columbia University's Bureau for Applied Social Research[2] found in their research on Jewish students, carried out in the years 1960 to 1964, that 13 percent abandon all connections with the Jewish community by the time they have reached their final year. It was discovered, however, that about half of them return, in one form or another, to the Jewish community within three years of completion of their studies. Further investigation in later years might very well show a further "return to the fold" as the one-time student faces the real world with its various social pressures.

Unfortunately, statistics on the dating patterns of young Jews are few and far between, although, significantly enough, they all indicate the same trend. In the Riverton study[3] Sklare and Vosc found that 62 percent of the Jewish teen-agers had no "close friends" who were gentile, 66 percent had "mostly Jewish" friends, and only 3 percent had "mostly gentile" friends; 43 percent of the adolescents old enough to date had dated non-Jews; 42 percent said they would not do so under any circumstances. Those who had dated non-Jews said that many of the parents had granted grudging approval, 40 percent having disapproved and another 40 percent expressing reluctant approval on condition that "nothing serious develops." A survey of 107 Jewish high school students conducted in New Orleans[4] showed that while a big majority had at some time "dated" non-Jews, only 16 percent had "gone steady."

Sanua[5] in 1965 studied 229 Jewish college students attending secular and religiously oriented colleges. Sixty percent of the secularly educated and 90 percent of the religiously educated declared that they never date a person of a different religion. Another study directed by Sanua in 1962[6] of about 180 Jewish teen-agers of 14 and 15 years of age showed that 23 percent of the girls and 40 percent of the boys had no objections about dating non-Jews – a very clear minority. Thirty-five percent of the girls and 21 percent of the boys would not date non-Jews. The rest, while not objecting, had reservations stemming either from a fear of the possibility of intermarriage in the majority of cases or from anticipated parental objections. For what it is worth, mention may also be made of the replies given to the author of this survey by forty-one American Jewish teen-agers (16 to 18 year olds). Asked how many of their four closest friends were Jewish, 20 replied that all four were Jewish and 10 stated that three were Jewish; 23 never date non-Jews, 15 sometimes, and only 3 did so regularly. While the sample is exceedingly small it has the advantage of including teen-agers drawn from all parts of the United States. These teen-agers were spending their summer vacation in Israel (1968) but this in itself does not make them untypical of American Jewish teen-agers in general. Approximately 50 percent were from the Zionist youth movement, Young Judea, but, interestingly enough, no significant differences were found between movement members and those who belonged to no movement.

A somewhat different result was obtained in Wilkes-Barre, Pennsylvania,[7] a community of about 5,400 Jews, where 225 teen-agers (121 boys and 104 girls) between the ages of 11 and 15 formed the sample. Only 16 percent agreed that "Jewish teen-agers should never date non-Jewish teen-agers." On being asked whether they did actually date non-Jews in practice, 61 percent answered affirmatively, a majority but considerably less than the 84 percent who in theory had no objection to dating non-Jews. There were no significant differences between the sexes. There is, of course, no indication of the intensity or frequency of these interreligious relationships. Furthermore, fully 80 percent had predominantly Jewish friends.

A recent survey taken in Pittsburgh[8] dealt, among other matters, with Jewish teen-agers' attitude to dating with non-Jews. Of the 326 teen-agers interviewed, 50.9 percent said that they did date non-Jewish persons and 49.1 percent said they did not. Of those who dated, 80 percent of the parents knew; 47 percent of the parents involved disapproved, 27 percent were indifferent, and 12 percent approved. Nearly 79 percent of all the teen-agers indicated that their three closest friends were Jewish, despite the fact that just over half dated non-Jews.

Parental attitude is an important factor. Caplowitz and Levy[9] in their sample of 520 students from an elite university in a big eastern city found that the Jewish students (50 percent, with equal sex distribution) were more influenced by parental attitude to interreligious dating than were Catholic or Protestant students. On being asked how they thought their parents would react to regular mixed dating, no less than 87 percent of the Jewish students thought that their parents would disapprove, as compared to 46 percent of the Catholic students and 55 percent of the Protestant students. Only 4 percent of the Catholics, 1 percent of the Protestants, and 1 percent of the Jewish students thought their parents would actually approve.

These are, of course, only assumptions on the part of the students. More significant is the response of these students to presumed parental attitudes. Here we are no longer dealing with assumptions about others but with the actual attitude of the students themselves. Seventy-six percent of the Catholic students, 70 percent of the Protestant, but only 47 percent of the Jewish students stated that in response to parental opposition they would continue the relationship and ignore their parents' objections. Twenty percent of the Catholics, 27 percent of the Protestants, and 40 percent of the Jews would "see that the relationship does not become serious"; 4 percent of the Catholics, 3 percent of the Protestants, and 13 percent of the Jews would discontinue the relationship in the face of parental objection. College experience tends to weaken religious ties and to free the children from parental constraint. The Jewish students seem most resistant to these liberating pressures. They tend to be much more aware of parental opposition to mixed dating and to be under some strain in the face of this pressure. Nevertheless, while 87 percent of the Jewish parents are assumed by their children to be opposed to regular mixed dating, only 13 percent would be prepared to discontinue the relationship.

The Caplowitz-Levy survey does not indicate any significant differences among the sexes as regards mixed dating. This is in sharp contradiction to the general practices of intermarriage, where it would appear that many more Jewish males marry out than do Jewish females. The study indicates that the children of academics are most likely to go in for inter-dating and that the children of lower class Jewish parents are least likely to. This is in accordance with the known trends of intermarriage among American Jews.

Several community studies have indicated parental attitude to interreligious dating. In Kansas City, Missouri,[10] 68 percent of the parents would disapprove if their child dates with non-Jews "most of the time" and 53 percent would approve if their children never dated non-Jews. The Bayville survey[11] indicated that 68 percent of the parents strongly disapprove of mixed dating and 23 percent mildly disapprove. In Baltimore[12] it transpired that while the majority of parents are desirous that their children should have social contact with non-Jewish children at school, there is a sudden change of attitude when the child gets into his middle teens. Sixty-five percent of parents of children 13 to 19 years old said that they will never agree that their child should date a non-Jew. The information available from the Wilkes-Barre youth survey is interesting because this is a small community with little more than five thousand souls, yet possessing a very strong community framework and a relatively high proportion of Orthodox families. Only 35 percent of the teen-agers thought that their parents disapproved.

What conclusions can be drawn from these scattered and fragmentary surveys? Inadequate as the material is, it appears that resistance to interreligious dating among teen-agers and particularly among parents is strongest where the Jewish community is large. Thus we find over 90 percent of the parents in the Greater Miami area disapproving, and one of the basic reasons for this is no doubt the fact that a majority of the Jews have their origins in New York. Likewise, we find greater resistance among Sanua's New York sample than among the youth of Wilkes-Barre (only 30 percent of the Orthodox youth disapproved of mixed dating!). Apparently, the smallness of the Jewish social framework makes it more difficult to oppose inter-dating and this is strictly in accordance with the known trends of intermarriage, which is considerably higher in smaller communities than in the big cities.

It is important to note that hesitancy over interreligious dating is not confined solely to Jews, although it is undoubtedly strongest among them. Gordon[13] undertook a large and comprehensive survey of 5,407 students in some forty colleges and universities. No less than 31 percent of the students rarely or never date students of other religions. Only 45 percent would continue to date someone they loved, belonging to another religion, unaffected by any doubts or hesitancy.

In all likelihood, interreligious friendship reaches its peak in the college years and for obvious reasons. Space does not allow us to survey what is known about

Jewish-gentile adult friendship patterns but the relatively large amount of material which exists on this subject indicates conclusively that Jewish adults invariably choose the big majority of their friends from among other Jews, regardless of the intensity of their Jewish consciousness. As Sklare and Vosc point out in the Riverton study, in a democratic society it is hard for the parents to express openly censure on this question. They prefer the more subtle strategy of selecting neighborhoods and activities which will foster association with other Jewish youngsters.

THE ATTITUDE OF THE YOUNGER GENERATION

Attitude and behavior are by no means the same thing, nor is the relation between them always a consistent one. This is particularly the case in such a delicate personal matter as intermarriage. A declared attitude one way or the other on the part of a young teen-ager or university student need not necessarily result in the appropriate behavior when it comes to the actual choice of partner. Nevertheless, there is obvious value in discussing the attitude of young people to this question while at the same time bearing in mind the above reservation.

Several surveys have been made in recent years of different groups of Jewish high school pupils in which they have been asked for their views on intermarriage. The New Orleans youth survey dealt with a group of 107 high school pupils. Seventy percent of those belonging to Reform congregations (the majority of the pupils came from a Reform background) said that a person should marry the one he loves without regard to religion, but only 35 percent of the non-Reform teen-agers agreed with this. The girls were less inclined to do so than the boys. This devotion to the American concept of "romantic love" coming before everything else did not prevent fully 80 percent of all the young respondents from believing that intermarriage is likely to lead to problems in the family. Moreover, 60 percent say that the Jew who intermarries should insist on the children being brought up as Jews.

The Wilkes-Barre youth survey of 225 young teen-agers indicated that in order to be a good Jew it is "essential" to marry within the faith. This was a view held by close on 60 percent, while the view that it was "desirable but not essential" was held by close on 32 percent. Eight percent were of the opinion that it "makes no difference." As in the case of the New Orleans survey, the girls were more convinced than the boys that intermarriage should be rejected, 65 percent of them believing it to be "essential" to marry within the faith in order to be a good Jew as compared with 54 percent of the boys who thought so.

Sanua[14] in 1966 questioned 133 high school boys and 56 high school girls in New York. The two groups were divided into those who had had a good Jewish education and those whose Jewish education had been weak. Among the boys,

60 percent of those with a good Jewish education said that they would strongly disapprove if a brother or sister of theirs were to marry a non-Jew, as compared to 35 percent who would disapprove among those whose Jewish education had been weak. Among the girls about 50 percent of both groups would disapprove. Less abstract and touching more on their own personal lives was the question whether or not they would break off at once a relationship with someone who they felt was "for them" if it transpired that the person involved belonged to another religion. Here we find quite a different picture, a far greater readiness to accommodate themselves to the possibility of intermarriage. In reply to this question only 20 to 26 percent of the boys answered affirmatively and between 17 to 42 percent of the girls, the higher figure denoting those who had had a good Jewish education. In all cases, less than half and in most cases less than a quarter would be prepared to break off the relationship.

In the Riverton study the adolescents were asked if they thought they could ever become really interested in a non-Jewish boy or girl (everyone understood this to mean "with a view to marriage"). More than half said they could not, while 37 percent said they could. However, as the authors suggest "these figures reflect simply an intellectual admission of a hypothetical possibility, rather than acceptance or desire." This qualification must be borne in mind in regard to teen-agers' attitudes in all the surveys. When asked how they would feel about marrying a non-Jew themselves, 70 percent indicated that they would not like it while of the remaining 30 percent many were uncertain. Forty-four percent said they would not want to marry out because they wished to remain Jewish and wanted to bring their children up as Jews; 21 percent said they would not feel right about marrying out because they knew that their families would disapprove.

In keeping with virtually all the surveys of old and young on the question of intermarriage we find, here too, in the Riverton study that, despite the big majority who reject intermarriage, the power of love is seen as overcoming everything else. Seventy-five percent would pick a non-Jew they were in love with rather than a Jew they were not in love with. The Pittsburgh study of 1967 indicated that 40 percent of the 326 teen-agers interviewed felt that it was essential to marry a Jewish person in order to be a good Jew. In other words, considerably less than half hold the opinion that in order to be a good Jew one should, among other practices, marry a Jewish person.

Finally, we would refer once again to the survey made by the present writer of American Jewish teen-agers who spent part of the summer of 1968 in Kibbutz Yas'ur. They were asked whether they considered intermarriage as "calamitous," "undesirable," "unimportant," "desirable." Of the 41 respondents the respective answers were 12, 23, 4, 2. Those who rejected intermarriage (the overwhelming majority) were asked their reasons for doing so. Fifty percent of the reasons given were connected with possible family troubles and difficulties in bringing up the children. The girls in particular gave this reason. Twenty-five percent of the reasons were connected with a desire to remain loyal to the Jewish people. Interestingly, only three teen-agers mentioned parental opposition.

Three trends stand out in the attitudes of all these teen-agers. First, intermarriage is rejected by the big majority but is seen more as being undesirable rather than calamitous. While it is not perhaps a completely fair question to posit "the non-Jew you love to the Jew you do not love," the overriding importance given by these youngsters to romantic love would indicate that their opposition is by no means absolute. Second, there is a clear-cut tendency in all the surveys for girls to be more hesitant about intermarriage than boys. The actual statistics of intermarriage do show that a smaller percentage of girls marry out than boys. Third, it would be unwise to exaggerate the effect of parental disapproval. This is undoubtedly an inhibiting factor, but the unclear and vacillating attitude of many parents and the foreknowledge that all will eventually be forgiven probably result in a dilution of the weight of this particular factor.

It has been variously estimated that there are approximately 350,000 Jewish students in American universities and colleges. All the evidence indicates that between 85 and 90 percent of Jewish boys and 60 and 70 percent of Jewish girls get a higher education. Yet there are few areas of Jewish life in America which have been so neglected from the point of view of research as the present-day Jewish student. It is generally assumed, correctly or otherwise, that the university experience encourages a more affirmative attitude to intermarriage on the part of the Jewish student. Whatever the case, it is certainly true that his links with the Jewish community are more tenuous than those of any other group of Jews. The evidence indicates that a similar process occurs among Catholic and Protestant students.[15]

The survey made by A. I. Gordon and published in his book *Intermarriage,* 1964, throws much light on student attitudes on this question. Gordon surveyed 5,407 students in forty colleges of whom 47 percent were Protestants, 31 percent Catholics, 12 percent Jews, 5 percent other denominations, and 5 percent without religious affiliations. The answers were not recorded in relation to the religion of the respondent and we cannot know exactly how the Jewish students responded. Nevertheless, the overall picture is of great interest. Ninety-one percent of all the students do not favor marriage to a person of another color, 50 percent do not favor marriage to a person of another religion (in the eight Catholic colleges included the percentage rose to 77), 31 percent, 16 percent, and 13 percent do not favor marriage with persons from other educational groups, nationalities, and different economic classes respectively.

The figure of 50 percent not being in favor of marrying a person of another religion is of particular interest to us. The average is brought up to 50 percent by the outstandingly high percentage of Catholics who hold this view. We have no means of knowing what percentage of Jewish students think this way, because the division is between types of schools only. Fourteen of the universities were State universities and here the percentage of those not in favor of marrying someone from a different religion was 45. The fifteen private universities produced the figure of 47 percent not being in favor. The vast majority of Jews attend State or private non-Catholic and non-Negro universities and there are no grounds for assuming that Jewish students would show more acceptance of interreligious marriages than do others. On the contrary, we are on fairly safe ground if we assume that Jewish disfavor is higher than the average and probably exceeds 60 percent.

Caplowitz' and Levy's survey of 1965 is more limited in scope than Gordon's but it has the advantage of religious classification thus enabling us to know exactly how the Jewish students responded. Of the 389 respondents, 50 percent were raised as Jews, 28 percent as Protestants, 14 percent as Catholics, 3 percent indicated some other religion, and 5 percent claimed to have been brought up in no religion at all. Ninety percent of all the students say that the rate of intermarriage is increasing, 9 percent say it is stationary, and 1 percent say it is decreasing. The figures are much the same for all the three main religious groups. If 90 percent of the Jewish students are of the opinion that intermarriage is on the increase, then this alone is a potent factor in encouraging intermarriage among the Jews. Seventy-one percent of the Jews, 75 percent of the Protestants, and 81 percent of the Catholics considered intermarriage easier today than it was ten years ago or were of the opinion that it was never difficult. The rest were of the opinion that it is just as difficult today as it was ten years ago. A minute 1 percent thought that the difficulties had actually increased. It is clear that such a general attitude is itself a stimulus to intermarriage.

Caplowitz and Levy found that their students were much more sensitive to class differences than religious differences when it came to the question of intermarriage. Thirty-six percent of the Jews, 20 percent of the Protestants, and 12 percent of the Catholics believed religious similarity to be important for marital happiness, while 64 percent, 80 percent, and 88 percent respectively considered same social class as being important. Although the Jews stress the religious aspect to a far greater extent than the Protestants or the Catholics, only a little more than one-third of them believe it to be important for marital happiness. Gordon's findings are in complete contradiction to those of Caplowitz and Levy. In his survey, religious similarity was considered by his students as being far more important than social or class similarity, and an average of 50 percent stressed the religious factor as compared to 27 percent in Caplowitz' and Levy's study. Whether this is due to the specific characteristics of Columbia University or to the general indecisiveness of such investigations we cannot say. At any rate it is clear that the Jewish student has more doubts on this issue than do others. Twenty-two percent of the Jews, 14 percent of the Protestants, and 11 percent of the Catholics believe that if a Jew marries a Catholic or a Protestant the couple will not feel as close as a Christian couple.

Of particular interest is the fear that children of a mixed marriage will suffer psychological problems of identity and that such marriages should be avoided for that reason. Sixty-four percent of the Catholics and 58 percent of the Protestants dismiss this objection to intermarriage but only 47 percent of the Jews are prepared to do so. Concern over the fate of their children is an important factor which causes the Jewish student to hesitate about intermarriage. Various investigations have shown that the Jewish family is usually more consolidated and wields more influence over its members than is the case with most other groups. Caplowitz and Levy found a direct relationship between the likelihood of intermarriage and parental attitude. Only 6 percent of Jewish students whose parents strongly disapprove of intermarriage said that it was likely that they would marry out compared to 15 percent of those whose parents were mildly disapproving only and 52 percent of those whose parents were indifferent. No doubt there are other factors involved here, such as a higher degree of Jewish consciousness among sons and daughters of parents who are opposed to intermarriage, but nevertheless the well-known Jewish family solidarity certainly strongly influences the children.

The most recent study known to us is that of Irving Jacks.[16] His was a study of 221 Protestant students, 233 Catholic students, and 192 Jewish students. Sixty percent of the Catholics and 54 percent of the Protestants were prepared to marry persons of other religions; 39 percent of the Jews said that they were prepared to do so, 31 percent were not prepared to do so, and 30 percent were not sure. Jacks found that second-year Jewish students were more prepared to consider intermarriage than were first-year students.

We must bear in mind that what we have been discussing up till now has been attitudes and not actual patterns of behavior. Not every Jewish student who boldly proclaims his right to marry a non-Jew will eventually end up by marrying one. Caplowitz and Levy remark that the actual rate of intermarriage is much smaller than the liberal attitudes and dating patterns of the Jewish student would lead one to believe. Yet there are obviously very serious grounds for concern for those who view intermarriage disapprovingly. Caplowitz' and Levy's final figures (percentages) are most significant [see following page].

Our information is so scattered and fragmentary that it becomes exceedingly difficult to know exactly what the real situation is. Contradictions abound. In 1965 Caplowitz and Levy investigating nearly four hundred Jewish students at Columbia found that 15 percent said that they were likely to marry out. Hershel Shanks[17] in 1953 investigated 350 Jewish students at the same university and found that 35 percent were likely to marry out.

LIKELIHOOD OF INTERMARRIAGE (Percent)

	Catholic	Protestant	Jew
Very or quite likely	66	46	15
Not too likely	28	43	47
Not at all likely	6	11	37
	100	100	100
Number in sample	50	99	188

It is, we believe, a mistake to assume that the tendency towards intermarriage which becomes so prevalent among Jewish students is the result solely of their exposure to the university climate. The roots go back much further. The lack of a real Jewish atmosphere at home and the inadequacy of Jewish education must be seen as the root causes. The Jewish student is inadequately prepared Jewishly for the university.

ATTITUDE OF PARENTS

In present-day American society the concept of "romantic love" rules supreme. This means, in theory, that all other factors such as religious affiliation, economic status, etc., are subordinate to this one overriding consideration, namely, "romantic love." In practice, matters work out very much differently but such is the theory. Furthermore, the concept of equality for religious, ethnic, and even racial differences is also theoretically accepted as part of the "American way of life." This is particularly so among Jews, of whom a larger than average percentage have been supporters of liberal views. These considerations, stemming from the theoretical premises of American life, naturally play an important role in determining the attitude of Jewish parents to intermarriage. Frequently they clash with strongly enrooted desires and instincts which are strongly opposed to intermarriage. In order to satisfy their conscience and to assure themselves that they are good Americans and behaving as good Americans should, Jewish parents frequently resort to various subterfuges in order to justify their opposition to intermarriage.

Such opposition is widespread and appears to be capable of producing the strongest emotions. It is regarded as the "point of no return," although in actual fact this is not always the case as the increasing number of conversions to Judaism shows. While the various surveys invariably indicate, as would be expected, a higher degree of opposition among Orthodox parents than among Reform, opposition is strong even among the very assimilated. The problem is further complicated by the fact that when it comes to marriage, most parents believe that their children have the right to choose their own marriage partner as they see fit.

A few examples will show clearly the high degree of opposition to intermarriage prevalent among Jewish parents. In the Kansas City survey 54 percent expressed strong disapproval and 20 percent mild disapproval; 13 percent were indifferent and 8 percent expressed mild or strong approval. A significant fact is that 66 percent of those adults whose parents were foreign-born strongly disapproved as compared to 23 percent of those with American-born parents. Sklare[18] in his important study of the suburb "Lakeville" in a big mid-western metropolis reported that 29 percent would feel very unhappy if their child were to intermarry, 43 percent somewhat unhappy, 24 percent indifferent, and 2 percent would feel happy. This is a well-to-do community with a higher than average Jewish income and from this point of view Sklare warns us that it is not typical of American Jewish communities although it may well be so in ten to fifteen years hence. Nevertheless, the big majority are opposed to intermarriage.

A recent community survey in Boston[19] provides interesting information.

ATTITUDE ON INTERMARRIAGE
OF ONE'S OWN CHILD ACCORDING TO AGE (Percent)

	Age Groups					
Attitude	21–29	30–39	40–49	50–64	65 plus	Total
Strongly oppose	15	18	28	36	31	26
Discourage	51	46	43	42	38	44
Be neutral, accept	29	26	25	21	27	25

This same study also shows a clear tendency for those who have gone to college and particularly graduate school to report greater acceptance of intermarriage, especially among the later generations. As this group is rapidly encompassing the big majority of Jews it is clear that there is a strong connection between higher education and acceptance of intermarriage which is likely to be of greater and greater importance as the years go by.

Another important fact emerging from the Boston study is the changing behavior of Reform Jews. Although all generations of Reform Jews are less resistant to intermarriage than Orthodox or Conservative Jews, the gap between them decreases with each successive generation. While 53 percent of Reform Jews born abroad would accept intermarriage, among third-generation American Reform Jews only 25 percent would.

In the Baltimore survey 207 parents of marriagable-aged children were asked what would be their reaction if their children married non-Jews. Sixty-seven percent would oppose it outrightly, 20 percent would express a reserved opposition; 5 percent said it made no difference to them and 3 percent said they would approve. In the Pittsburgh Jewish youth survey, 69 percent of the parents would strongly disapprove if their child intermarried and 16 percent would mildly disapprove. The older the child the higher the percentage of those who strongly disapproved.

The above examples are typical, we believe, for American Jewry. Opposition is widespread. Younger American-born parents are more inclined to oppose "mildly" rather than "strongly." This, we believe, is due more to the influence of American societal norms than to an actual lessening of opposition. It is just not "done" in present-day American society to "strongly oppose" your son's wishes, especially when they are so obviously in keeping with accepted American concepts. There is undoubtedly the fear of alienating the child by excessive opposition.

The Boston study indicates a small reduction in opposition to intermarriage among those over the age of 65. While the differences are not great they throw a certain amount of light on an interesting psychological aspect of the problem. When it comes to marriage, many Jewish parents feel that the fault will be theirs should their child choose a non-Jewish partner. There develops a feeling of guilt that they have not succeeded in inculcating their child with an adequate or satisfactory attachment to his people and his religion. The over 65s are presumably grandparents and the direct responsibility for the young person is not theirs. Freed thereby from the feeling of any guilt they are not infrequently able to adopt a less disapproving attitude.

In the previously mentioned Lakeville study, Sklare found that only 14 percent of those who oppose intermarriage explicitly based their opposition on a concern for Jewish survival, identity, or religion. They prefer to stress that discord is inevitable and that intermarriage is inherently unstable. The Boston survey showed that 53 percent agree that intermarriage is bad for the Jewish people, 34 percent do not think so, and 13 percent have no opinion. However, the relationship between considering intermarriage bad for the Jewish people and opposition to your own child intermarrying is by no means a consistent one. Only slightly over 50 percent of those who would "discourage" a family intermarriage consider that it is bad for the Jewish people, and, on the other hand, 20 percent of those who would not resist their own child's intermarriage do consider it bad for the Jewish people.

Some indication of the way in which Jews evaluate intermarriage can be gained from some of the Jewish communal surveys made in recent years. In the Kansas City survey of 1961 the respondents were asked what is obligatory for a good Jew. Fifty-three percent said marrying within the faith. It was eleventh on the list. Among Jews born outside the United States 66 percent mentioned this but among third-generation Jews and later generations still, the percentage dropped to 14.

The Lakeville study discloses that 23 percent consider it "essential" for a good Jew to marry within the faith, 51 percent say it is desirable, and 26 percent say that it has no bearing on the question of being a good Jew or not. In Essex County[20] (1961) a little less than 50 percent considered it necessary for a good Jew to marry only a person of the Jewish faith. In "Southville"[21] a large southern metropolis (1959) 53 percent considered it essential for a good Jew to marry within the faith, and in Baltimore (1963) 55 percent thought so. These five surveys show a considerable degree of uniformity on this question, between 50 and 60 percent considering in-marriage essential for a good Jew.

The stress which many Jewish parents place on the purely personal aspect of the problem, namely, possible family discord, the difficulties of raising children, etc., is used as an excuse to avoid emphasizing ethno-centrism which is looked upon with suspicion and distrust by many of the younger generation. Widely approving the American ideal of complete integration the parents try to find a respectable alternative to the disinclination to sanction what is the ultimate in interfaith and interethnic acceptance. The "personal" aspect fulfils this function. It enables the parents to satisfy tradition and their own feelings and instincts without endangering their acceptance of American democracy.

The most potential threat to the Jewish defence against intermarriage lies in the American ideal of "romantic love." In the Lakeville study, Sklare found that 85 percent preferred their children to marry a non-Jew who was loved rather than a Jew who was not. There is no factor so powerful as "love" and American Jewish parents find it difficult to compete against it. Significantly, in a choice between a non-Jewish doctor or lawyer and a Jewish carpenter, 29 percent would prefer the former as their son-in-law and 54 percent the latter (Lakeville study).

There is no doubt that the big majority of American Jewish parents do not want their children to marry non-Jews, but gone are the days when parents will sit "shiva" for a child who has married out. When the inevitable has happened, the parent will reconcile himself to the position, especially if there has been a conversion to Judaism. American acculturation and the consequent drop in Jewish consciousness have led to the disappearance of the trauma and rupture which would have been the case several generations ago. On the other hand, the desire for family cohesion is sufficiently strong to make for a reconciliation. Young Jews presumably know this and so the fear of causing a family crisis and a break between the generations becomes progressively less and with it the inhibition against intermarriage. The young American Jew knows that eventually "the folks will get used to it."

THE RATE OF INTERMARRIAGE

Religion is not one of the items included among the census questions in the United States, and consequently when people get married their religious affiliation is not recorded by the authorities. Thus, we have no nationwide figures dealing with the number of Jews who marry non-Jews. One exception is the two States of Iowa and Indiana, which do record the religious affiliation of those who marry. Unfortunately, neither of these states has a large Jewish population but the statistics available for these two states have been analyzed by Erich Rosenthal and will be dealt with by us further on.

The only information we have of a nationwide character is that acquired through the religious census of 1957. This was the first and only census ever taken by the US government which included a question of religious affiliation. Thirty-five thousand families were included in this experimental census, among them 1,100 Jewish families. The Census Bureau found that only 7.2 percent of Jewish heads of households were married to non-Jewish spouses. The comparable figures are 8.6 percent among Protestants and 21.6 percent among Catholics. A few words of warning are needed here, most of which are applicable not only to this particular government census but to practically all the local surveys. In the first place, the Census Bureau itself reported that its statistics on intermarriage were probably subject to a larger margin of error than is usually the case because, although the surveyors were asked to ascertain whether the spouse was of the same religion as the head of the household, many of them arbitrarily assumed that the religion mentioned by the head of the household was the religion of the whole family.

A weakness common to this census and to most other local surveys lies in the fact that the recorded religious affiliation is that which is held at the time of the interview. It is not known how many persons belonged to a different religion before their marriage and then converted. The figure of 7.2 percent of Jewish family heads whose spouses were not Jewish does not include those whose spouse was originally not Jewish. There is of course a world of difference between those marriages in which the non-Jewish spouse has become Jewish and those in which they have maintained their original non-Jewish religion. Nevertheless, it would be interesting to arrive at the overall figures, which, unfortunately, are generally not available. The 1957 religious census deals with family heads, the overwhelming majority of whom are presumably men. What of the Jewish women, who are not family heads, and who have married non-

Jewish husbands? The percentage will certainly be lower than the 7.2 percent of Jewish family heads who had non-Jewish spouses, as it is a well-known fact that fewer Jewish women marry out than do Jewish men. This would result in the overall percentage of all Jewish persons, male and female, who had married non-Jewish spouses being lower than the above mentioned 7.2 percent.

A third weakness of this government census and of some, but by no means all, of the local surveys, is that it deals with the ratio of intermarriage and not the rate. All marriages of all age groups are included. This can lead to a grave misunderstanding of the present situation. It is obvious that among the older generation, many of whom were born in Eastern Europe, the degree of intermarriage will be much less than among present-day young college graduates. To lump them all together will certainly provide a ratio, an average, but it will give us no indication of the present rate of intermarriage which is of decisive importance. Marshall Sklare[22] writes: "The current rate, then, may well be at least double that of the Bureau's cumulative ratio. And even the cumulative ratio is bound to soar in the decades ahead with the thinning out of the ranks of those who are presently keeping it down - first and second generation Jews."

The most comprehensive survey is that of Erich Rosenthal[23] in which he deals with Jewish intermarriage in the State of Iowa and in Greater Washington. Rosenthal bases his study on the findings of the Greater Washington Jewish Communal Survey published in 1956. Of the 23,313 households in which at least one spouse was Jewish, 86.9 percent were marriages in which both partners were Jewish and 13.1 percent were those in which one partner was Jewish and the other non-Jewish. This is almost double the 7.2 percent of the Census Bureau, which is most probably on the low side for reasons already mentioned, and is in similar sharp contrast with previous local surveys, which had also usually noted a similar figure. That the 13 percent level of intermarriage is not an anomaly resulting from the unique character of Washington as the nation's capital, with its large and mobile professional and white-collar workers, will become evident as we proceed. Unlike other communities which in their surveys had limited themselves to master lists of Jewish families known to them and consequently more involved in Jewish life, the advantage of the Washington survey lies in the fact that in addition to utilizing the name lists of different Jewish organizations a cross-section of the total Washington population was made, resulting in the relatively high level of 13 percent.

For the first time - to the best of Rosenthal's knowledge - an attempt was made to demonstrate the relationship between generation and intermarriage. Among the males the level of intermarriage in the first generation (foreign born) was 1.4 percent, the second generation (natives born of foreign parents) 10.2 percent, and among the native-born of native parents (the third and subsequent generations) 17.9 percent. Thus we see that while the general ratio of intermarriage was 13 percent, the current rate was as high as 18 percent.

The Providence survey[24] of 1964 found that 4.5 percent of the Jewish heads of the family had married non-Jewish spouses. However, 39 percent of the non-Jewish spouses had converted to Judaism, so that in actual fact the percentage of household units in which one member was Jewish and one member non-Jewish was as low as 2.7 percent. This represents an exceedingly low ratio of intermarriage but fortunately the survey provides generational details which enable us to arrive at the present rate of intermarriage. In the 20 to 29 age group the percentage was 9, in the 30 to 39 age group 1.7, in the 40 to 49 age group 7, and among the over 60s it was 1.3. There is no clear explanation for the big drop in intermarriage in the 30 to 39 age group but nevertheless, the tendency for the rate to increase with each successive generation is obvious, despite the one exception. The current rate of intermarriage in Providence is 9 percent as compared to a general ratio of 4.5 percent.

The Boston survey of 1967 indicated a higher rate of intermarriage. Seven percent of all marriages consist of one partner who is not Jewish. The breakdown for the different generations is as follows: among the 30 and under age group there are 20 percent of such families; 31 to 40 age group, 7 percent; 41 to 50 age group, 7 percent; and in the 51 and over age group, 3 percent. Thus the current rate of intermarriage is no less than 20 percent compared with 18 percent in Washington, 9 percent in Providence, and 7.2 percent in the national census.

The Rochester survey[25] of 1961 shows that 8 percent of all households where the head was Jewish had one member who was not born Jewish. Due to conversion the actual ratio was 5.3 percent. No figures are available for different generations, so we cannot know the current rate. The Camden survey[26] of 1968 shows a general ratio of 5 to 6 percent. The San Francisco survey[27] of 1959 shows a very high level of intermarriage, amounting to 17 percent in the city itself and reaching up to 37 percent in the suburbs. The most recent survey of a large community that we are aware of is that of Los Angeles[28] (1968) giving an overall figure of 5.4 percent. Unfortunately, in these last four surveys no breakdown for different generations is given and we do not know the current rate, which is certainly far higher.

As previously mentioned, Iowa and Indiana are the only states in the United States which collect information on the religious affiliation of brides and grooms. Jewish intermarriage in Iowa was the subject of a study by Erich Rosenthal.[29] Iowa has a total Jewish population of a little over nine thousand. During the seven years between 1953 and 1959 the average yearly rate of intermarriage among the Jews was 42.2 percent and in the last year of 1959 it had risen to 53.6 percent. In this case, we have not got the general ratio but only the more important current rate. Iowa, of course, is not typical of American Jewry, consisting mainly of very small Jewish communities.

Rosenthal also made a study of Jewish intermarriage in the State of Indi...
In the four-year period, 1960-1963, 785 marriages involving Jews took place. The yearly average of intermarriages was 48.8 percent with 49.1 percent in 1963. These latter figures represent the current rate. Once again, as in the case of Iowa, it must be pointed out that Indiana is not typical of American Jewry, consisting mainly of small communities with a total population of something over twenty-three thousand. The obvious relationship between the rate of intermarriage and the size of the community will be discussed further on.

The examples that we have taken do not show a clear-cut picture as to the ratio or current rate of intermarriage today in the United States. The figures vary greatly. On one point, however, all the surveys agree. With each successive generation the rate increases. The present young generation of under 30s is marrying out to a far greater extent than did previous generations.

SOCIOLOGICAL FEATURES

An outstanding feature in all surveys of Jewish intermarriage, not only in America, is the fact that a far larger number of Jewish males marry out than do Jewish females. Even in our discussion of dating patterns and pre-marital views on intermarriage we found a greater degree of disapproval among Jewish girls than among Jewish boys. Rosenthal in his study of Greater Washington found that out of a total of 3,051 intermarriages, 69 percent involved Jewish husbands and 31 percent Jewish wives. These figures do not differ greatly from those obtained by the same author in Iowa, where intermarried Jewish men constituted 76 percent and Jewish women 24 percent of all those who had intermarried. The Camden survey indicated that 84 percent of all intermarriages involved Jewish men and only 16 percent involved Jewish women. Rosenthal, in his study of Jewish intermarriage in Indiana, found that exactly twice as many males as females married out. Gordon in his study of Minneapolis Jewry[31] found that in nearly all cases of intermarriage it is the Jewish youth who marries the non-Jewish girl. And so on. The evidence is overwhelming.

According to Simpson and Yinger[32] there is a general tendency for the men of a racial, religious, or ethnical minority to marry out to a greater extent than the women. It is suggested by them that the factors responsible for this tendency are: (1) the women in these groups have fewer opportunities for meeting men in the majority groups than do the men belonging to the minority groups; (2) religious and parental control may have a stronger influence on minority women than on minority men; (3) men take the initiative in dating and courting; (4) increased status for the minority male who marries a woman from the majority group. Whether these factors apply to the Jewish minority today in America can well be a matter for discussion. In contrast to the tendency for Christian wives to carry the main responsibility for religious education, Judaism gives the primary religious role to the male, although from the halachic point of view a Jewish child must have a Jewish mother. Perhaps the male-centeredness of the Jewish religion results in more Jewish males marrying out than Jewish females. It may be easier for them to maintain their religious and ethnic identity in a mixed marriage.[33]

On the other hand, the weight of the evidence must not blind us to the possibility that our assumption requires considerable modification. Owing to the dominant position of the male in modern society it is possibly easier for him to maintain his religious and ethnic identity. We do not know how many Jewish girls marry non-Jews and lose their religious and ethnic identity, thereby ceasing to exist from the point of view of Jewish statistics. The Jewish households of Greater Providence contain only a minute proportion of couples in which the husband is non-Jewish by birth. The report found, however, that 4.3 percent of all the females are married to non-Jews as compared to 4.5 percent of the males. This discrepancy lends support to the thesis that a considerable number of Jewish women marry out and become lost to the Jewish community and are therefore not included in those surveys which focus only in the identifiable Jewish households.

A second feature which is typical of intermarriage is the relationship between the degree of intermarriage and the density of the Jewish population. The level of Jewish intermarriage is lower in the large Jewish community than in the smaller ones. In the very small Jewish communities the old adage "familiarity breeds contempt" comes into force and the combination of local exogamy and social disorganization brings about a situation in which intermarriage becomes an accepted tradition among small-town Jews.[34]

The Iowa study by Rosenthal illuminates this point very clearly. In the seven-year period studied from 1953 to 1959 intermarriage in cities with a population of over ten thousand amounted to 34.2 percent of all Jewish marriages, in towns with a population of 2,500 to 9,999 they amounted to 64.1 percent, and in rural areas to 67 percent. The average for the state as a whole is 42 percent. In his study of Jewish intermarriage in Indiana Rosenthal found that in the five major Jewish communities one-third of the marriages were out-marriages as compared to two-thirds in the remaining counties. Rosenthal's Washington study likewise provides confirmation. The intermarriage rate for life-long residents of Greater Washington is 14.9 percent, considerably more than the 11.7 percent among immigrants originating from larger Jewish communities, mainly New York, Baltimore, Philadelphia, Boston, and Chicago. The enormous rate of intermarriage in small communities is no doubt typified by Charleston, West Virginia,[35] a Jewish community of some 1,300 souls. During the ten years from March 1, 1959, to February 28, 1969, 61 percent of the Jewish males who married did so with non-Jewesses and 17 percent of the Jewish women who married in this period did so with non-Jewish males. The overall rate of intermarriage during this period was no less than 40.4 percent, a figure which corresponds very closely with that given by Rosenthal for Iowa, 42 percent. The percentage of intermarriage couples in the community as a whole rose from 18.4 percent in March 1959 to 26.7 percent in February 1969. The rate of intermarriage in this small community is rapidly accelerating. Between March 1968 and February 1969 of eight Jewish males who married, only one did so to a Jewish girl. The authors of this survey mention that to the best of their knowledge there were no conversions among the non-Jewish partners.

Several studies on intermarriage among Catholics demonstrate the same tendency. Intermarriage among Catholics in the South where they are comparatively few is far higher than in New England where they constitute 50 percent of the population. The paucity of the Jewish population is not by itself sufficient to cause the increase of intermarriage in smaller communities as compared to larger ones. In pre-Hitler Germany, for example, intermarriage was far more frequent in the cities. Such intermarriage as there was in Poland and Lithuania (about 1 percent) was almost totally confined to the cities. The decisive factor is the degree of Jewish social and religious cohesion, which several generations ago was stronger in the small communities of Central and Eastern Europe than in the big cities. In present-day America, however, a small community is synonymous with a loose and disintegrating Jewish social and religious framework.

Hardly any research has been done on the relationship between education (both secular and Jewish), occupation, income, etc., and the rate of intermarriage. The only studies which investigate these aspects of the problem are those by Rosenthal on Washington and Iowa. The Washington survey provides some valuable and surprising information concerning the relationship between higher secular education and the rate of intermarriage. Among the foreign-born Jews those whose education had gone furthest had the highest rate of intermarriage; those with between 13 and 16 years of education had 1 percent intermarried while among those whose education had extended for seventeen years or more the figure rises to 4.1 percent. The difference is between that of college graduation only and graduate study.

The picture is completely changed when we turn to the second generation (native-born of foreign parents) and even more so in the third and subsequent generations (native-born of native parents). In the second generation those with college graduation only had among them 15.6 percent who had intermarried while those who had had a still higher education, graduate training, had among them only 11.4 percent who had intermarried. Among the third generation the difference is far greater, the equivalent figures being 37 percent and 14.9. The current rate of intermarriage among those with the highest education, graduate training, is well less than half of that of those with a lesser education, college graduation only. This highly unexpected finding is also paralleled by a rise in traditional identification among those with a higher education. Rosenthal's opinion is that the explanation for this unexpected relationship between graduate education, level of intermarriage, and degree of Jewish identification will be found in an examination of the relationship between group identification and occupational choice. A further factor involved may, in our opinion, be the higher age of those with the highest education. With the increase in age there may be a tendency to consolidate Jewish ties.

Occupational choice among American Jews is widening. Discrimination and the desire for group survival in the past led to a very high degree of self-employment in business and in the professions. This is still the case today but to a lesser degree. Occupational homogeneity facilitates social contacts which can lead to marriage within the group. The Washington survey brings out very clearly that those who are self-employed have a lower level of intermarriage than those who are employees. Nor are government employees more prone to intermarriage than are other employees, as has been frequently thought. On the contrary, among the native-born there is a slightly lower level of intermarriage among government employees as compared to other types of employees.

In our opinion, occupational structure plays a very important role in influencing the level of Jewish identification and intermarriage. The fact that intermarriage is lower among the self-employed in the Washington sample is probably no coincidence. It is quite likely that many self-employed Jews, particularly those in business, are dependent on, or at any rate closely collaborate with, their families. Business is frequently done with other Jews. Jewish professionals frequently have a predominantly Jewish clientele. Such an occupational structure tends to draw Jewish people together, as Rosenthal points out, thus reducing the likelihood of intermarriage. A further result could well be the realization that intermarriage is "bad for business." Most Jews prefer a Jewish doctor or a Jewish lawyer and the existence of a non-Jewish wife could possibly be detrimental to the Jewish businessman or professional. Such considerations play no particular role in the case of employees.

Rosenthal's study of Jewish intermarriage in Iowa emphasizes this point even more clearly. Among Jewish grooms in first marriages, 29.6 percent were intermarried, but among managers, proprietors, and officials (many of whom are self-employed) the rate is as low as 10.3 percent. All white-collar workers combined have an intermarriage rate of 27.2 percent while blue-collar workers (of whom many will be employees) have, by contrast, a rate of 46.8 percent.

The Washington study shows clearly that the intermarried had, on the average, a higher income than others. The foreign-born intermarried male had an income 3 percent higher than foreign-born Jews who had married Jewish wives. Similar figures apply to such cases among native-born sons of foreign parents but in the third and subsequent generations, in other words, the present-day generation, we find the gap much larger. The average income of those in this group who are intermarried was in 1956, $10,386, 30 percent higher than the average of $7,965 among those of this group who had not intermarried.

The Washington data confirm the generally held belief that Jewish education serves as a check on the rate of intermarriage - in the third generation at least. Among those latter who had had no religious education, 30.2 percent were intermarried compared to 16.4 percent among those who have had some Jewish education. The second generation, the native-born of foreign parents, presented a completely opposite picture. Among those who had had some Jewish education 11.1 percent were intermarried compared to 4.1 percent of those who had no Jewish education. Thus it would appear that Jewish education does have an inhibiting effect on the rate of intermarriage, at least as far as the present generation is concerned. However, the whole question of the influence of Jewish education on the future Jewish identity and consciousness of the adult has been severely neglected. Rosenthal suggests that in view of the enormous weakening of ethnic ties in the third generation, the religious bond alone holds the members of the group together and thus religious education helps to reduce intermarriage.

A question of vital significance is that concerning the children. Are they brought up as Jews or non-Jews? The Washington survey revealed that in 73 percent of all the mixed families the children were being brought up as non-Jews, in 17.5 percent of the families the children were being brought up as Jews, and in 9.5 percent of the families some of the children were being brought up as Jews and some as non-Jews.

The Camden survey of 1964 indicates that in those mixed marriages where there had been no conversion, one-third of the children were being brought up as Jews and two-thirds as non-Jews. These figures corroborate those of Washington, although in the latter case the figures relate to the percentage of families and not of children. Whether the basis is the number of families or the number of children makes very little difference. Earlier investigations recorded identical phenomena. Fishberg[36] says that all the evidence points to the tendency for the big majority of children of mixed marriages to be brought up as non-Jews, about 75 percent being brought up as Christians. Ruppin[37] states that in an extensive survey taken in Prussia in 1910, only 23 percent of all children of mixed marriages were being raised as Jews.

Contrary evidence comes, however, from the Providence survey. Here it was found that among couples in which the non-Jewish partner had not converted, 84 children were being raised as Jews and 60 as non-Jews. The children mentioned here do not include those who were not living at home and therefore refer mainly to young children and to young families. The importance of this finding is by no means minimized, however, by this reservation. Completely contemporary trends are always of decisive importance.

The Providence findings notwithstanding, there is a very logical basis for the claim that the majority of children in mixed marriages, where the non-Jewish partner has not converted to Judaism, are being brought up as non-Jews. The big majority of Jews who marry out are males. This means that in a mixed family the father is most likely to be Jewish and the mother non-Jewish. In present-day American society there are no norms concerning the religious identity of children born of mixed marriages but usually they follow the religion of the mother. In Jewish law it is not a matter of choice; the child is Jewish only if the mother is. It is quite natural that generally speaking the child's religious identity should be that of its mother and this would account possibly for the larger number of children in mixed marriages who are brought up as non-Jews. All this applies only to families where there has been no conversion.

Conversion from one religion to another is an increasingly common phenomenon in contemporary America. The social importance of religious affiliation and the lack of importance attached to theological belief are prime factors for this tendency. The modern family seeks harmony in the religious sphere; those whose religious beliefs are very important to them will probably not marry out. The Providence report indicated that 39 percent of the non-Jewish spouses had converted to Judaism. While only a third of the non-Jewish spouses in mixed marriages involving the foreign-born converted to Judaism, among the third generation it was over 50 percent. In the Camden survey a third of the non-Jewish spouses had been converted. Goldstein and Goldscheider[38] analyzing the findings of the Providence survey found that in those cases in which the husband was over 60 none of the non-Jewish spouses had converted; of those in the 40 to 59 age group 40 percent of the non-Jewish spouses had converted, and in those cases in which the husband was under 40, the figure rose to 70 percent.

The evidence is admittedly meager, but it may well be that an increasing number of non-Jews are converting at the time of marriage. The considerable decrease in anti-Semitism and the improved status of the Jews in American society are possible factors of influence. Despite the increase in conversion there is no question that the Jewish community loses more than it gains from intermarriage.

PROBLEMS AND RESULTS

As we have seen the argument that intermarriage creates problems in personal and family relationships is the chief weapon of many parents in their attempt to dissuade their children who may desire to marry non-Jews. This argument is probably used to a greater degree than the one of safeguarding Jewish survival.

Most of the evidence available appears to indicate a higher rate of family mishaps among intermarried couples. Zimmerman and Cervantes[39] compared divorce rates among mixed and unmixed marriages in five cities. They found that in all five cities the rate of divorce and desertion among mixed marriages was higher than among non-mixed couples. In Boston, for example, where both parties were Protestant the rate of divorce and desertion was 7.3 percent but rose to 11 percent when only the husband was Protestant. Among Jews in Boston the rate was 4.7 percent when both partners were Jewish but rose to 25 percent when only the husband was Jewish. A similar situation was found among the Jews of New Orleans.

In a recent article by A. S. Maller mention is made of a recent study by Christenson and Barber of marriage and divorce records in Indiana of all couples married in 1960 and divorced within the next five years. Catholics and Jews had a divorce rate 79 percent and 69 percent below the average respectively. However, Catholics who married non-Catholics had a divorce or annulment rate five times as high as those who had married within the faith, and for Jewish mixed marriages the rate was six times as high as that among all-Jewish marriages.

Most of the more recent studies dealing with Protestant-Catholic marriages have found a greater rate of divorce among mixed couples than among couples of the same religion, although according to the very comprehensive study of Burchinal and Chancellor[40] based on records of the State of Iowa, it would seem that the rate of broken marriages was more influenced by the lack of religious identification of the non-Catholic partner than by a school of religious values and beliefs. To what extent this is applicable to intermarriages where one of the partners is Jewish is not demonstrable, unfortunately.

Berman[41] puts forth the interesting suggestion that people who are intermarried are more likely to be divorce-prone without this indicating that there is a higher percentage of unhappy marriages among intermarried people than among those who are not. Berman reasons that among intermarried people there is a higher than average number of rebels. They ignore society's disapproval of intermarriage and in the same fashion are more prone to flaunt society's disapproval of divorce.

The fate of children born of a mixed marriage and the difficulty they find in adopting a clear-cut ethnic and religious identity has been a subject for much descriptional work and polemics. We have, however, been unable to find any study comparing children, both of whose parents were Jewish, with children who had only one parent Jewish. The Roston[42] study of 1960 dealt with students already at college. Roston studied a group of fifteen Harvard and Radcliffe students, "mischlings" – as Roston calls the children of a mixed marriage.

All fifteen students had one parent Jewish and the other non-Jewish. None of the fifteen regard themselves as Jewish but all but one said that society as a whole regards a half-Jew, half-gentile as a Jew, regardless of the individual's own preference. The sample under study was embittered against the parents for not having prepared them adequately to deal with the attitudes of their status groups towards Jews and towards "mischlings." To what extent, however, the norms of Harvard and Radcliffe can be considered as being typical of present-day American society is debatable, at the very least.

Undoubtedly, the question of religion for the children represents a major stumbling block in intermarriages. Conversion of one parent may reduce the problem but any other solution is rife with conflicts. Whether, as in some cases, all the children were brought up in one religion or whether the religion chosen by the parents depends on the sex of the child; whether the parents agree to let the child himself decide when he grows older to what religion he belongs; or whether it is decided to maintain a religious void in the family, all these various solutions are likely to confuse the child and make him feel insecure. The same applies equally to the cultural and ethnic identity of the child. Much descriptive material on the types of problems which the children incur is to be found in Gordon's book, *Intermarriage.*

The realization that intermarriage may lead to problems for the children may possibly have an influence on the birth rate among intermarried couples. Goldstein and Goldscheider in their analysis of the Greater Providence Jewish Population Survey of 1964 report certain differences in the birth rate of intermarried couples as compared to families in which both partners are Jewish. Twenty-six percent of the older-aged mixed families were childless as compared with 9.7 percent of fully Jewish families of the same age-group. This very considerable difference is reduced among the younger married couples. In this generational group 14 percent were childless among the intermarried as compared to 8 percent among the fully Jewish families of the same age-group. For both age-groups the difference is significant.

That the difference in percentage of childless marriages among younger families (intermarried as compared to intramarried) is less than the differences found in the older age-group may well indicate that the stigma of intermarriage is less strong and that younger people feel less apprehensive about the problems facing children of mixed marriages. This is also borne out by the fact that unlike older generations there was only a slight difference in the younger group in regard to the number of children in a mixed marriage and in a fully Jewish one. The slight difference may be due to the tendency of people marrying out to be a year or two older than the average.

There are many consequences to intermarriage, both on a personal and social level. Relations with in-laws and the more extended family must vary tremendously and we are not aware of any quantitative studies which would enable us to generalize. The social framework of a mixed couple is also likely to be different. Gans[43] in his well-known study of suburban life mentions that non-Jewish friends of Jews in Levittown usually had Jewish spouses. It would be far beyond us to attempt to postulate any generalizations concerning the personal and social status of Jewish intermarried couples today in the United States.

On the other hand, there is a not inconsiderable literature describing the feelings and emotions of various individuals and the problems, both personal and social, which they face. In addition to Gordon and Berman whose books contain many "live stories," valuable insight into the problem can also be got from John Mayer[44] and from Levinson and Levinson[45] who made a study in depth of sixteen mixed couples.

CAUSES OF INTERMARRIAGE

Under this heading we refer to sociological and psychological motivation. In these spheres we cannot base our argument on quantitative surveys, which to the best of our knowledge are not available, and that for obvious reasons. We can do no more than note the observations and assumptions of sociologists and psychologists. In doing so, it should be remembered that our survey is concerned with Jewish intermarriage, while the concept of intermarriage itself is much wider. It includes not only marriage between people of different religions (not only Jews) but also marriages between different racial groups (negroes and whites, etc.), different national groups, and even persons of different economic and social classes. Theoretically, any marriage which is not based on complete homogeneity can be termed an intermarriage. As our interest here is only with Jewish intermarriage, generally understood to mean marriage between a Jew and a person of another religion or of no religion, at any event, a non-Jew, we shall endeavor to deal with those factors only which seem relevant to our own theme.

A number of general propositions favoring intermarriage and which certainly apply to Jewish intermarriage, should be mentioned. Numerous studies have shown that there is a strong relation between marriage and residential propinquity. Despite modern communications and increased mobility, these studies show that approximately 25 percent of all marriages are contracted by people living within five blocks of each other and 50 percent are contracted by people living within twenty blocks of each other. Jewish ghettos or Jewish quarters are to be found in all big cities of America but they are no longer exclusively Jewish. Practically all "Jewish" districts have a large percentage of non-Jews living in them. This is particularly so in the suburbs to which more and more

Jews are flocking and must surely be considered an important factor causing intermarriage.

Maller in two recently published articles[46] raises a point whose importance should not be underestimated. Many Jews may marry gentiles because they have difficulty in the Jewish "marriage market" and not necessarily because they are "liberal." In the previously mentioned Christenson and Barber study of Indiana it transpired that while 20 percent of Jews who had married Jews had previously been married, no less than 38 percent of Jews who were married to non-Jews had previously been married. This would indicate that there is more likelihood of intermarriage occurring in the second marriage than in the first. The proportion of Jews who ranked high in occupational and educational status was 25 percent lower for those involved in a mixed marriage and this was true for both Jewish grooms and brides. As might be expected from the higher proportion of previously married, the age of those involved in mixed marriages was about two years older at the time of marriage than the average age of an all-Jewish couple at the time of marriage. Thus, being older, divorced, and of lower occupational status are directly related to Jewish mixed marriages.

Maller points out that various studies indicate that the socio-economic class of those who marry out is frequently below average, as exemplified by the Iowa study of Rosenthal. One common complaint of Jewish males is that Jewish girls are too demanding. The upward mobility of the Jewish community results in an increasing number of upper middle-class Jewish girls excluding themselves from the Jewish marriage market because they are not willing to marry "down." The percentage of unmarried female college graduates is double the percentage of all unmarried adult women in the United States.

Every year 20 percent of Americans change their place of residence.[47] The degree of Jewish social mobility is certainly not below average. This results in younger people being more and more exposed to people of different backgrounds. It also leads to a weakening of established control groups.

The Jewish economic structure is changing. While maintaining and even consolidating their predominant middle-class character, they are now penetrating new fields to an ever-increasing extent. Government employment started on a large scale during the New Deal days of Roosevelt. The ever-increasing participation of Jews in academic life is a post-Second World War phenomenon. The decrease of anti-Semitism on the one hand and the ever-increasing range of federal and local government employment are resulting in more and more Jews becoming employees and at the same time leaving the more traditional Jewish occupations. This in itself is a powerful factor in favor of intermarriage.

The salaried professions usher the Jew into a gentile world quite different from that of the Jewish businessman or independent Jewish doctor or lawyer. This new world is largely gentile and extremely mobile. Ties with the family and with the community are weakened, frequently severed. Kramer and Leventman[48] write that the professional man is considered a "lost cause" by Jewish community leaders. They are highly mobile and are not generally attracted to the organized community unless they have older children. For a variety of reasons this type is more in rebellion against the Jewish Establishment and all it stands for than any other group in the Jewish world. As Rabbi Richard Rubenstein[49] puts it: "Should his enthusiasm for his intellectual world be shared by a young woman of another faith, there is little that could hold him to Jewish life." And it is precisely this class and type which is rapidly growing among young American Jews!

Marshall Sklare[50] reports on a recent (at that date) study conducted by Rabbi Henry Cohen.[51] According to this study approximately 20 percent of the Jewish faculty members of the University of Illinois - well over twice the national average - are married to non-Jewesses and this is a conservative university with a large Jewish student body whose parents sent them there in order to avoid the perils of intermarriage! The Jewish population of Champaign-Urbana (the university is situated here) numbers about 250 people divided equally between town and university. Rabbi Cohen found a 20 percent ratio among the Jewish townspeople. The contrast between town and university is even more startling because most of the Jewish faculty members were sons of East European immigrants and had been brought up in predominantly Jewish neighborhoods while many of the townspeople were already third and fourth generations in America.

Other examples of the rapid progress of intermarriage among Jewish intellectuals could be given but the point involved is not so much the quantitative aspect but the fact that the behavior of the Jewish faculty on the campus undoubtedly has considerable influence on the young Jewish student and this behavior is quite saturated with intermarriage. Intermarriage thereby acquires a degree of respectability and can even serve as an example to the Jewish student. As close on 90 percent of Jewish males attend college the importance of this factor can hardly be underestimated.

The general tendency of the young generation to leave the traditional Jewish occupations with their strong Jewish family and Jewish social associations and the shift to the salaried professions combine to make the changing Jewish occupational structure one of the most potent causes of Jewish intermarriage. Jews are now working with gentiles as colleagues instead of serving them as merchants and professionals.

A new factor making for intermarriage is the change in the attitude of the non-Jew. Intermarriage is increasing not only because the Jew is moving out more and more into general society but also because the tastes, ideas, cultural preferences, and life-styles professed by many Jews are more and more becoming to be shared by non-Jews, as Sklare notes. Rubenstein, in his above mentioned essay, remarks that in the course of "emancipating" themselves many of the bright middle-class non-Jewish girls are attracted by the political liberation characteristic of Jewish students and by their equally characteristic avantgardism in intellectual and aesthetic matters. The Jews have achieved in America today a delicate balance between conformity and non-conformity, between acceptance and marginality. The average well-educated gentile girl does not want too much of a Bohemian for a husband but nevertheless would like someone who is "different." The Jew fits this category admirably.

In general, the marked rise of egalitarianism, the growing suppression and rejection of prejudice, the decrease in anti-Semitism, and the improved status of the Jew are potent influences making for intermarriage. To which must be added the developing acculturation of American Jews, the weakening of Jewish religious and ethnic identity, and the increasing disintegration of traditional family controls as factors which further encourage intermarriage. On the whole we would venture the hazard that the single most important factor in the sociological sphere is the growing acceptance and status of the Jew in present-day American society.

Probably the most important depth analysis of the psychological aspects of Jewish intermarriage is the study by M. M. Levinson and D. J. Levinson which appeared in the Yivo annual of 1958. Sixteen intermarried couples with 11 Jewish husbands and 5 Jewish wives were the subject of a small-scale, intensive, psychologically orientated study to determine the types who intermarry and the reasons which prompted them to do so. The Levinsons found two types: those who intermarried despite their own opposition to the concept and whom the Levinsons called "the reluctants," and those to whom intermarriage was in keeping with their social values and whom the Levinsons styled "the emancipated."

The "emancipated" intermarried as part of a general process of assimilation having its cause partly in the family and social environment. Particularly for the men it was a result of a strong and largely successful struggle for emancipation from infantile ties. The unconscious Oedipal conflict seems to have been adequately solved and the subjects were fully mature people. Intermarriage was consistent with their values and ideology. "In terms of psychological dynamics their marriage choice is not 'symptomatic' in the neurotic sense; it has important adaptive and ego-integrative functions for them."

While there were no internal personality conflicts among the "emancipated," the case of the "reluctants" represented an attempt to solve a neurotic conflict. Although disapproving of intermarriage in principle, they had, nevertheless, done so. "Emotionally they were fixated in their intense and ambivalent relationships with their mothers and had great difficulty establishing adult independence. Their intermarriage ... was a form of 'neurotic exogamy,' that is, it represented an attempt to solve a neurotic conflict regarding hetero-sexual relations."

The Levinsons, as well as other students of intermarriage, have remarked on the inability of certain men, who eventually intermarry, to form a relationship with Jewish women. The psychological analysis of the Levinsons offers an explanation of this phenomenon and indicates deep-rooted causes of intermarriage. The participants were asked to describe their conception of the "good wife" and also their estimations of their mothers and sisters, and in most cases there was a sharp contrast. Jewish women were seen "as more emotionally demanding and dominating." In the big majority of cases the mother was the dominating figure in the home and was described as "nervous."

It would seem that the well-beloved "Jewish mother" is a not insignificant factor in causing intermarriage, even among those who are in principle opposed to it and have a fairly developed Jewish identity.

In his interesting study of Jewish-gentile courtships, Mayer sought to identify the factors which led an individual to marry someone who has previously been considered ineligible. There are cases in which the individual eventually chose a partner - a non-Jewish one - although previous to the marriage he disapproved of intermarriage. On the basis of his interviews Mayer found that the following factors were highly influential in bringing about a marriage of "reluctant" with "ineligible": (1) whether the disability of the "ineligible" becomes known immediately (awareness of ethnic and religious identity at time of introduction); (2) whether the latter has certain characteristics which compensate for this disability; (3) whether "reluctant" feels confident that the relationship will not go "too far"; (4) whether "ineligible's" disability can be changed (conversion); (5) whether those who disapprove of the relationship fail to prevent its progress; (6) whether those who oppose the relationship conceal their disapproval or at least refrain from actively intervening; (7) whether there are present any conditions which will insulate "reluctant" from whatever negative pressure is brought to bear; (8) whether the influence of those who disapprove will be stronger than those who approve.

Mayer points out that in spite of their denial of any intention to marry, as a couple continues to see each other they become more deeply attached and increasingly cut off from other prospective marital partners. Friends and family become increasingly tolerant and accept the fate which the partner himself has been loath to recognize. Instead of making a decision in the face of an unsympathetic society, he finds himself conforming to the expectations of others. "Everybody says we are going to get married, so we might as well go ahead and do it."

In addition to the above set of inter-personal relations, Mayer finds that working together or studying together seems to provide the best conditions for the development of mixed marriages. In addition to the light which they throw on the psychological causes of intermarriage, the studies of the Levinsons and of Mayer are important because they deal with Jews who prior to their marriage with a non-Jew were opposed to intermarriage. We cannot, of course, say what percentage of those Jews who intermarry do so despite their original disapproval of such marriages and their incipient reluctance to enter into such a partnership, but their numbers must be considerable. It would seem that assimilation and a weak Jewish identity are by no means the only causes for assimilation.

The aim of Jerold Heiss'[52] study was to define those characteristics of family and religious experience which reduce the normal barriers to intermarriage. Heiss' survey of 1.167 persons in Manhattan (12 percent of whom were Jews, a lower percentage than the Jews of Manhattan constitute) disclosed that, in general, the intermarried are characterized by: (1) non-religious parents; (2) greater dissatisfaction with parents when young; (3) greater early family strife; (4) less early family integration; (5) greater emancipation from parents at time of marriage. While all these five characteristics were found among the Catholics, only (4) was strongly represented among the Jews with (5) receiving some support. Heiss suggests that "intermarried Jews differ from intramarried Jews only in the strength of their family ties while young and at the time of marriage." It would appear that among Jews early familial experience of a distressing kind is likely to be one of the causes of intermarriage. One either seeks a partner resembling the parents or one seeks a partner differing in certain ways from them.

Several other hypotheses which suggest unconscious psychological forces have been advanced. Most of them have not been tested empirically. Three theories, in particular, have in the past achieved considerable popularity but their relevance today is somewhat doubtful. The first theory suggests that intermarriage is a form of status-seeking. The minority person, unable to achieve acceptance in the majority society, seeks to identify with it by means of intermarriage, thereby improving his own status. The second theory sees intermarriage as a form of hostility to parents. By intermarrying the child unconsciously punishes the parents. The third hypothesis suggests that intermarriage is a form of escape from anti-Semitism and from the burden of being Jewish. In his article in *Commentary* April 1964, Marshall Sklare criticizes each of these theories on the grounds that they are no longer relevant to the Jewish position in present-day America. Discrimination is on the wane and the difficulties of being Jewish are today much less than was the case a generation or two ago. Being Jewish is becoming less and less an obstacle to personal progress, so that while in the past these features may have been among the more important causes of intermarriage their relevance today is doubtful. Of the second theory concerning hostility to parents Sklare says: "Were this theory particularly pertinent, one would expect Jewish-gentile marriages to be most prevalent in the second generation, where the trauma of acculturation was most decisively experienced and the generational conflict was at its most intense." The fact is, however, that intermarriage rates are clearly higher in the third generation.

Heiss' analysis of the Manhattan study supports this conclusion. Surveying the mental health rating assigned to each respondent by a board of psychiatrists, he found that there was no significant difference between the mean rating achieved by those who had intermarried and those who had not.

Maria and Daniel Levinson conclude their study with a few pertinent observations which appear to be reasonably well established: "... intermarriage is not ... a unitary phenomenon. It occurs under a variety of psychological and social conditions and has varying consequences. Psychologically, it is not purely a neurotic manifestation, although neurotic motives may enter to varying degrees. Nor is it to be seen solely as an "escape" from the Jewish group or as a means of securing social or financial gain, although motives of this kind play a part in some cases."

As Sklare says, it is precisely the "healthy" modern intermarriage which raises the most troubling question of all for the Jewish community.

INTERMARRIAGE AND THE FUTURE OF THE JEWISH COMMUNITY

The earliest study of Jewish intermarriage in America is that of Julius Drachsler whose book, *Democracy and Assimilation,* published in 1920, received a good deal of attention at the time of its publication. Taking the years 1908 to 1912 as his base, Drachsler found that in New York City the Jewish intermarriage rate was a mere 1.17 percent. American Jewry was relieved to learn that intermarriage, in New York City at any rate, was no great problem.

Twenty-five years later the results of another study were published and once more American Jewry was satisfied to learn that the Jewish reputation for endogamy was a justified one. Ruby Jo Reeves Kennedy[53] found that for all the years investigated - 1870, 1900, 1930, 1940 - Jews in New Haven had the lowest intermarriage rates of all ethnic and religious minorities. Kennedy developed the theory that while ethnic groups were merging, this process of assimilation was taking place within the framework of the three main religions of America, Protestantism, Catholicism, and Judaism. While no longer marrying to any great extent in their own ethnic group, Americans usually married within their religious group and this, presumably, would be the future pattern of American society. In the 1950s Will Herberg[54] made extensive use of this theory.

The American Jewish public was reassured and little attention was paid to the problem of Jewish intermarriage. The government religious census of 1957 was a further source of comfort; 7.2 percent of marriages involving Jews were found to be intermarriages. The actual percentage of individual Jews (as distinct from the percentage of marriages) who had married non-Jews was found to be as low as 3.7 percent according to the 1957 census. We have already commented on the limitations of this census. Nevertheless, these figures, if we accept them at their face value, certainly give the impression that intermarriage among Jews is relatively very limited. Glick,[55] on the basis of the government census, made the interesting calculation that on a purely chance basis 98.2 percent of all families involving Jews should be mixed ones and that 96.4 percent of all Jewish individuals would marry non-Jews. In view of these calculations the actual figures of the census were seen as being most gratifying and reassuring.

The publication in the 1963 *American Jewish Year Book* of Erich Rosenthal's study of intermarriage in Greater Washington was a highly significant landmark. Not only did it provide much new information concerning the relationship between education, income, occupation, etc., and rate of intermarriage but by making abundantly clear the distinction between ratio of intermarriage and rate of intermarriage it put an end to many illusions and self-deceptions. Rosenthal showed that while the overall ratio of Jewish intermarriage was "reasonable" the actual rate among the younger generation, namely, those actually marrying at the present time, was far higher. Since then we have been witnessing an increasing interest in the subject. Each of the three main Jewish denominations has devoted conferences to this problem in the last few years; the Federation of Jewish Philanthropies of New York held two full conferences in 1964 and 1966 and published detailed reports; in 1963 appeared "Intermarriage and Jewish Life," edited by W. Cahnman and consisting of papers read at a conference convened by the Herzl Institute. This was the first book on the subject to be sponsored by any American Jewish organization. The American Jewish Committee[56] published an excellent survey reviewing existing research, Marshall Sklare wrote his by now much quoted essay for *Commentary*, important books and essays have appeared by Gordon, Berman, Rosenthal, Sanua and others, all within the last couple of years - and we have by no means exhausted the list. Intermarriage has become one of the burning topics for American Jewry. It is at the top of the agenda together with the problem of Jewish education, and the interesting point is that there is virtually complete agreement that intermarriage is growing, will continue to grow, and represents a great danger to the future of the Jewish community.

How much do we really know about Jewish intermarriage in the United States? To what extent do the various local surveys reflect the situation in the country as a whole? The only thing that we can be really certain of is that we know very little. There has never been a nationwide survey of American Jewry; one is being prepared now, planned to encompass a representative sample of twenty-five thousand families. The result will not be known until 1971 at the very earliest. Our knowledge, therefore, of what is exactly happening in the sphere of Jewish intermarriage is extremely limited. Even the evidence of some of the well-known surveys has been disputed. The conclusions drawn from Rosenthal's basic study of Washington have been challenged on the grounds that Washington is not a typical Jewish community because of the high percentage of government employees and the consequent high degree of mobility. Rosenthal, on his part, states that he sees no reason for doubting the typicality of his findings. Recently, Rabbi David Eichhorn[57] has sought to cast doubt on the accuracy of Rosenthal's Iowa study, in which the latter brings figures to show that the rate of intermarriage among Jews is over 42 percent. Rabbi Eichhorn received information in 1967 from nine rabbis in the State of Iowa with an average length of service of ten years (three rabbis were excluded because they were new). These rabbis had as members of their congregations about 50 percent of all Jews in Iowa. Of the 551 marriages in their communities 9.3 percent were intermarriages. He argues that if we are to accept Rosenthal's figures, among the 50 percent who were not members of these nine congregations the rate of intermarriage has reached 75 percent, which is highly unlikely.

In the same article Eichhorn challenges the generally accepted belief that Jewish males marry out to a greater extent than do Jewish females. We ourselves have already dealt with some reservations which should be applied in connection with this theory. Rabbi Eichhorn is a Reform rabbi, one of the relatively few who are prepared to consecrate a Jewish marriage without the non-Jewish partner converting, and he states that since 1964 he has officiated at 428 mixed marriages in which 204 were Jewish men and 224 Jewish women.

Despite the above reservations it seems to us that the generalizations made in the course of this survey are basically correct. Despite the likelihood of a larger number of Jewish women abandoning completely their religion and ethnic identity than is the case with Jewish men, the evidence of numerous surveys indicates clearly that the degree of intermarriage among males is higher than among females. Nor can there be much doubt that with each successive generation the rate of intermarriage has increased. Once again the weight of the evidence is overwhelming. We must add, however, that while this has most certainly been the case up till now and including the present generation, it does not necessarily follow that this will be the pattern for future generations. Of this, more further on.

Victor Sanua estimated in 1967 that Jewish intermarriage was approximately at the rate of 17 percent. There are no means of checking this figure. It accords with the rate as found in large communities such as Washington and Boston although Heiss in his Manhattan sample found a ratio of 18 percent intermarriage among Jews and this means that the present rate is considerably higher. On the other hand, there are surveys which show a lower rate.

Taking Sanua's estimate as a rough yardstick and thereby assuming that intermarriage is now making considerable inroads into Jewish life, what can we say at this stage about the future? Will successive generations continue to intermarry at an ever-increasing rate, or have we already reached the highest point? In the course of our survey we have already dealt with some of the more important factors encouraging the growth of intermarriage such as parental tolerance or at least reconcilement, the changing economic structure of American Jews, the flow to the colleges and universities, the growing tendency in American society to be more liberal in these matters (especially in the universities), the growing weakness of Jewish ethnic and religious identity, etc. Have we any good grounds for assuming that these contributing causes are likely to disappear in the future or even to become weaker? For this to happen presupposes a radical change in American society. Will an increase in anti-Semitism (always a possibility) result in a drop in Jewish intermarriage? John Mayer in his book *Jewish-Gentile Courtships* observes that the relationship between anti-Semitism and intermarriage is not a simple one. A rise in anti-Semitism could possibly cause young Jews to seek an escape from the burden of being a Jew. The rise of Nazism in Germany did not stop intermarriage on a big scale until the Germans made it illegal, by which time to be even associated with a Jew was dangerous. A milder rise in anti-Semitic feeling may not necessarily reduce the rate; it can possibly even increase it. This, of course, is only a theoretical possibility and nothing more. It certainly cannot be tested. Will the growth of Black Power and Negro separatism create a reconsolidation of all the existing ethnic groups? Whatever modifications may take place in American society as a result of resurgent black nationalism, and there certainly will be such modifications and Jews will and already are bearing the brunt of these modifications, it is extremely unlikely that they will result in a remoulding of American life on basically ethnic lines with the incalculable effect this would have on the rate of intermarriage.

Yet certain changes, mostly within the Jewish community, are taking place and while we cannot know at present what effect they will have on the intermarriage rate, they are worthy of consideration. It is conceivable that some of these changes may slow down the rate or keep it at the present level.

The Jews in America are a more homogenous group than ever before. German or Russian or Polish origin plays little role. The differences in life-style between Orthodox, Conservative, and Reform Jews are rapidly decreasing. The overwhelming majority are college educated, live near each other, and are concentrated in the same occupations and professions. The degree of acculturation is very much the same for all. The dividing line between Jew and Jew, very severe a couple of generations ago and less, is disappearing. The result may be more in-marriage. As C. Bezalel Sherman[58] remarks "... as a group achieves social and economic equilibrium, the inclination of its members to marry outside the faith tends to taper off. If this holds true for the Jewish group, then we should expect the growing stability of the Jewish community to serve as a brake on intermarriage. There is no question that but for this growing stability the number and proportion of intermarriage would by this time have been higher." In our opinion, Sherman is mistaken in emphasizing social and economic equilibrium as factors making for a decrease in intermarriage, as the Catholic experience shows. If instead of emphasizing "social and economic equilibrium" we substitute "homogeneity," we believe that we shall be closer to defining an internal Jewish social characteristic which may have some influence.

Another factor, although far more problematic, but worthy of consideration, is the growing similarity between Jew and non-Jew. That fascinating and attractive "difference" between Jew and gentile, which led many to seek their partners outside the fold, is becoming less powerful as the process of acculturation deepens. Paradoxically, the very assimilation of young Jewish people may make them less attractive to non-Jews while on the other hand the young Jew may be less attracted to the gentile for the same reason.

That the changes that have occurred in Jewish occupational structure, increasing numbers of salaried professionals in non-traditional Jewish occupations, are an important factor making for intermarriage has already been mentioned. But how far can these changes go? Are we not approaching the stage beyond which Jewish economy will not go? This is one sphere in which the influence of Negro nationalism may well be felt by Jews. The openings in the field of "salaried professionals in non-traditional Jewish occupations" are not unlimited and Negro competition is likely to increase. If this is the case then while the occupational factor will continue to operate its potency will not grow. Much the same can be said of the students. A recently published study by Joseph Zelan[59] shows that religion is abandoned by a greater percentage of students in elite colleges than in other schools. This applies also to the Jewish students. Jews already account for a large percentage of the studentship of the elite Ivy League universities (Columbia 40 percent, Harvard and Yale, 25 percent each, with the other four Ivy League schools not far behind). This percentage is not likely to rise; there are indications that it will drop. If such be the case intermarriage would not necessarily drop, but this particular factor at any rate would not increase in potency.

Will these changes in American Jewish life actually result in a drop or at least a steadying of the rate of intermarriage? In our opinion no final judgment can at this stage be made. Apart from the inherent difficulties involved in measuring the actual force of each of these factors we need far more information and knowledge of Jewish life in America before we can permit ourselves to draw final conclusions.

NOTES

1 Milton M. Gordon, *Assimilation in American Life* (Oxford, 1964).
2 Preliminary Report in *Tefutsot Israef,* June-July, 1968, American Jewish Committee, Jerusalem.
3 M. Sklare, and M. Vosc, *How Jews Look at Themselves and Their Neighbors* (American Jewish Committee, 1957).
4 *A Study of Jewish Adolescents of New Orleans* (Jewish Welfare Federation of New Orleans, August 1966).
5 V. Sanua. "Intermarriage and Psychological Adjustment," in H. Silverman, ed., *Marital Counseling: Psychology, Ideology, Science* (Springfield, Ill., 1966).
6 V. Sanua, "A Study of Attitudes of Adolescents Attending Jewish Community Centers in New York," *Journal of Jewish Communal Service,* XLI (Summer 1965).
7 *The Jewish Teen-agers in Wilkes-Barre* (American Jewish Committee and Wilkes-Barre Jewish Community Center, 1965).
8 *A Summary of a Survey of Opinions of Jewish Teen Members of the Pittsburgh Y-ike* (American Jewish Committee and Pittsburgh Y.M. and W.H.A., November 1967).
9 D. Caplowitz, and H. Levy, *Interreligious Dating among College Students* (Bureau of Applied Social Research, Columbia University, 1965).
10 M. Shapiro, *The Kansas City Survey* (American Jewish Committee, 1961).
11 *Survey of Dade County, Greater Miami Area* (American Jewish Committee, New York, 1961).
12 M. Shapiro, *The Baltimore Survey* (American Jewish Committee, New York, 1963).
13 A. I. Gordon, *Intermarriage* (Boston, 1964).
14 Victor Sanua, "Jewish Education and Attitudes of Jewish Adolescents," in *Educators Assembly Year Book* (New York, 1967).
15 A. M. Greely, "Influence of the Religious Factor on College Students," *American Journal of Sociology* (May 1963); Harvard *Crimson,* June 6, 1959.
16 Irving Jacks, "Attitudes of Students to Intermarriage," *Adolescence* (Summer 1967).
17 H. Shanks, "Jewish-Gentile Intermarriage," *Commentary* (October 1953).
18 M. Sklare, and J. Greenblum, *Jewish Identity on the Suburban Frontier* (Basic Books, 1967).
19 *A Community Survey* (Combined Jewish Philanthropies of Greater Boston, 1967).
20 A report conducted by the National Research Opinion Center on the philanthropic patterns of the Jewish community of Essex County, New Jersey.
21 *A Survey of the Jewish Community of "Southville"* (American Jewish Committee, 1959).
22 M. Sklare, "Intermarriage and the Jewish Future," *Commentary* (April 1964).
23 *American Jewish Year Book,* vol. LXIV (1963).
24 S. Goldstein, *The Greater Providence Jewish Community: A Population Survey* (The General Jewish Committee of Providence, 1964).
25 *The Jewish Population of Rochester, New York* (Jewish Community Council of Rochester, New York, 1961).

26 C. F. Westoff, *A Population Survey* (Greater Camden County, Jewish Community, 1965).
27 F. Massarik, *The Jewish Population* (Jewish Welfare Federation of San Francisco, 1959).
28 *A Report on the Jewish Population of Los Angeles* (Jewish Federation Council, 1968).
29 E. Rosenthal, "Studies of Jewish Intermarriage in the United States," in *American Jewish Year Book,* vol. LXIV (1963).
30 E. Rosenthal, "Jewish Intermarriage in Indiana," in *American Jewish Year Book,* vol. LXVIII (1967).
31 A. I. Gordon, *Jews in Transition* (University of Minnesota Press, 1950).
32 E. G. Simpson, and J. Milton Yinger, *Racial and Cultural Minorities* (3rd ed., New York, 1965).
33 Robert Blood, *Marriage* (New York, 1962).
34 R. Shostack, *Small Town Jewry Tell Their Story* (B'nai Brith, 1953).
35 "The Jewish Population of Charleston, West Virginia," *11th Annual Report,* March 1969.
36 M. Fishberg, *The Jews* (New York, 1911).
37 A. Ruppin, *Jewish Fate and Future* (London, 1939).
38 S. Goldstein, and C. Goldscheider, "Social and Demographic Aspects of Jewish Intermarriage," *Social Problems,* XIII (Spring 1966).
39 C. C. Zimmerman, and C. F. Cervantes, *Successful American Families* (New York, 1960).
40 C. B. Burchinal, and C. E. Chancellor, "Survival Rates among Religiously Homogamous and Interreligious Marriages," *Social Forces,* XLI (1963).
41 Louis A. Berman, *Jews and Intermarriage* (London and New York, 1968).
42 "'The Mischling': Child of the Jewish-Gentile Marriage," honors paper submitted to Department of Social Relations, Harvard University, 1960.
43 Herbert Gans, *Levittown* (New York, 1967).
44 John Mayer, *Jewish-Gentile Courtships* (New York, 1961).
45 Maria H. and Daniel J. Levinson, "Jews Who Intermarry," *Yivo Annual of Jewish Social Science,* XII (1958).
46 A. S. Maller, *Jews and Intermarriage, Jewish Spectator,* February 1969; "New Facts about Mixed Marriages," *The Reconstructionist,* March 23, 1969.
47 Donald Bogue, *The Population of America* (New York, 1959).
48 J. Kramer, and S. Leventman, *Children of the Gilded Ghetto* (New Haven, 1961).
49 R. Rubenstein, "Intermarriage and Conversion on the American Jewish Campus," in W. Cahnman, ed., *Intermarriage and Jewish Life* (New York, 1963).
50 M. Sklare, "Intermarriage and the Jewish Future," *Commentary,* April 1964.
51 Henry Cohen, "Jewish Life and Thought in an Academic Community," *American Jewish Archives,* XIV (1962).
52 Jerold Heiss, "Pre-marital Characteristics of the Religiously Intermarried in an Urban Area," *American Sociological Review* (February 1960).
53 R. J. R. Kennedy, "Single or Triple Melting Pot? Intermarriage Trends in New Haven 1870-1940," *American Journal of Sociology,* XLIX (January 1944).
54 Will Herberg, *Protestant, Catholic, Jew* (New York, 1955).
55 P. Glick, "Intermarriage and Fertility Patterns among Persons in Major Religious Groups," *Eugenics Quarterly* (March 1960).
56 Sybil H. Pollet, *Marriage, Intermarriage, and the Jews* (American Jewish Committee, 1966).
57 D. H. Eichhorn, "Jewish Intermarriage," *The Reconstructionist*, December 6, 1968.
58 C. Bezalel Sherman, "Demographic and Social Aspects," in D. Janowsky, ed., *The American Jew* (Philadelphia, 1964).
59 Joseph Zelan, "Religious Apostasy, Higher Education, and Occupational Choice," *Sociology of Education* (Fall 1968).

BENJAMIN SCHLESINGER

Family life in the kibbutz of Israel

In 1969 the population of the State of Israel was 2,841,100, of which 2,434,800 were Jews, 300,800 Moslems, 72,150 Christians, 33,300 Druzes and others. About 3 percent of this population (84,200 persons) lived in the 235 kibbutzim or collective villages, with sizes ranging from sixty to two thousand people. The first kibbutz, Degania, was founded in 1909.

Though many kibbutzim run sizeable industrial enterprises, they are predominantly agricultural. All property in a kibbutz is collectively owned and work and living arrangements as well as the rearing of children are collectively organized. As the kibbutz was founded by middle-class European intellectuals for the purpose of rebuilding a Jewish nation, self-labor was highly stressed as a spiritual goal and as a means of self-realization. Hired labor, conceived as a way of exploitation of the worker, was completely discarded. Property used by the entire community rightfully belongs to the whole community. Individuals own nothing but a few personal gifts and have a small yearly allowance. Clothes and houses are distributed to the members with no preference shown for one individual over another. Different kinds of labor are not ranked or rewarded according to communal contribution, and everyone, regardless of his work, is viewed as a "worker." Nevertheless, social prestige exists and is achieved only by those who are productive workers. Another principle underlying the culture of the kibbutz is individual liberty achieved through freedom from the artificial conventions of an urban civilization. Freedom of reading and speech are equally emphasized. A last moral postulate is the emphasis on subordination of individual interests to the interests of the group.

The founders of the kibbutzim were predominantly of Polish and Russian origin, and their European experience influenced the kind of community they established. Eastern European Jews had lived in a world of anti-Semitic discrimination for a long time, and even in the schools, which were opened to them later, Jewish students were made to feel that they were strangers.

The culture of the Polish and Russian Jewish village or *shtetl* (small town) produced people who were caricatures of natural and normal men, both physically and spiritually, and was viewed unfavorably by the new generation. As a result, opposition to the parental way of living was openly expressed by the youth. The Zionist movement, with its values of love of nature, love of a nation, self-expression, and emphasis on the emotional aspects of life, soon became a model to be imitated and a means of emancipation from the bonds of urban mores and artificial convention. Return to nature and the ascetic life included simple housing, simple clothing, and avoidance of make-up by women.

Zionism, apart from its original ideology of an escape from Judaism and the culture of the shtetl, involved also the migration to Israel. In the early 1900s when ninety Jews arrived in the Israeli countryside, physical conditions were so harsh that many found it impossible to adjust and either returned to Poland or went to live in the cities; those who remained founded the kibbutzim. Hardships, lack of comfort, and strenuous physical labor resulted in close relationships, mutual support, and strong cooperation.

The roles of the traditional parental figures were also changed in the new "Utopia." The father not only does not rear the child, but he has no specific responsibility for him. The child is provided for by the kibbutz as a whole: he receives his food in the dormitory dining room, his clothes from the dormitory storeroom, his medical care from the dispensary, and his housing in the children's dormitories. The parents have little responsibility for the physical care of their children, nor does the family have the function of education and socialization, as children are subjected to the system of collective education which arose as a function of the kibbutz protest against the patriarchal father.

The kibbutz also attempted to change the woman's role in the family. Because woman must bear and rear children, she has had little opportunity for cultural, political, or artistic expression. If she could only be freed from this time-consuming responsibility, as well as from such other domestic duties as cleaning, cooking, and laundry, she would have time to devote to other interests and would become the equal of man. In other words, the crux of the problem was to be found in the emancipation of the woman from the yoke of domestic service. By instituting a system of communal socialization, it was believed, it would be possible to achieve part of this goal – the emancipation of woman from the burden of child rearing. And if her children were reared by professional nurses, the woman would not only be free from that responsibility but also she would be spared the chores of housekeeping since she and her husband would require little room.

Her complete "emancipation," however, included the abolition of all domestic chores. This was accomplished by the various communal institutions of the kibbutz: the communal laundry, kitchen, and dining room relieved her of the chores of laundry, cooking, and dishwashing.

Four days after giving birth in the hospital, the mother returns with her infant to the kibbutz. The child is placed there in the infants' dormitory with fifteen other infants ranging in age from four days to approximately one year. He remains in charge of a head nurse, who usually has received specialized training in child care. Since the infants are not taken to the parental rooms until they are six months old, almost all their physical needs, with the exception of nursing, and many of their emotional needs as well are satisfied primarily by their nurses. The mother breast-feeds the child at the same time she plays with him and tucks him into bed. The father sees the infant only after work and during the free visiting hours on Saturdays and holidays.

The first important change in the child's life occurs at six months when the infant may be taken by his parents to their room for an hour every afternoon. The second important change occurs at about one year when the child is moved from the infant's dormitory to the toddlers' dormitory where he must learn to adjust to a new building, a new nurse, many new children, a new routine, and a new discipline. In this dormitory the child is usually toilet trained, is taught how to feed himself, and learns to interact with his age mates. At this age he can stay with his parents for two hours in the evening and on Saturday. Between the ages of two and three the group acquires a nursery teacher who, like the nurse, cares for the physical and emotional needs of the children but is primarily in charge of their social and intellectual development.

At about four years the child encounters another important change, kindergarten, which involves his moving into a new building with an enlarged group of children and acquiring a new nurse and a new nursery teacher. The enlarged group will remain together until its members enter high school. After spending a year or two in the kindergarten the children pass into the "transitional class" where for one year they receive formal intellectual training before moving into the grammar school. School marks an important transition in the life of kibbutz children: it is the beginning of their serious intellectual training, it expands their interactional group to more children of different age levels, and it introduces them into formal responsibility and work.

Instruction in the school, which is based almost entirely on the project method, is conducted in an informal manner. Children have a voice in choosing the curriculum. There are neither exams nor grades, and passing is automatic – no one fails. At the completion of the sixth grade, at the age of twelve, the children graduate into the combined junior-senior high school. This is also an important transition in their lives for three reasons: (1) for the first time they encounter important male figures other than their fathers, because teachers now are primarily males; (2) the group splits up and the children form new groups comprising children from the cities as well as from their own kibbutz and from other kibbutzim; and (3) they begin to work in the kibbutz economy from one and a half to three hours, depending on their age.

The high school curriculum reflects the self-image of a socialist society of farmer intellectuals. There is practically no vocational or home economics influence in the entire curriculum. The focus instead is on the humanities, sciences, and arts, with much emphasis on the social implication of knowledge.

To the obvious criticism that children should not be separated from their mothers as they are in the kibbutz, there are two convincing rebuttals. First, with the exception of a very few cases almost invariably occurring among children entering the kibbutz at an advanced age, no bad effects have been observed, while, on the contrary, many good ones have resulted. Second, the well-to-do mother in private life habitually hands over her children to the care of nurses from the earliest age and usually sees them only at prearranged periods when she and they are at leisure; this is precisely what happens in the kibbutz, whose children are, in fact, treated just like those of the wealthy. This is true in the material sense too. Although as far as the adult members are concerned the kibbutz must limit the standard of goods and services, practically nothing is denied to the children, who are the pledge of the future on whom depends the fate of the kibbutz society. Consequently, the expenditure on the housing, clothing, feeding, and care of the children is far in excess of adult standards and is not infrequently increased at the expense of all other budget items. For children, the kibbutz is, in any case, a paradise; supervised by expert nurses they spend their early years playing and learning in interesting and pleasant rural surroundings. It is not surprising that kibbutz children are known throughout the land as prime specimens of Israeli youth.

This is not to say that there are not a good many difficulties in connection with their upbringing as in the case of children everywhere - difficulties both psychological and physical, requiring special attention. Cooperation between parents, nurses, teachers, and the doctor is easier and closer in the kibbutz than it can ever be outside. There is no difficulty in making special arrangements suggested by experts. Instead of the limited resources of the individual family, the much larger economic capacity of the whole kibbutz stands behind each child and parent. Mothers whose children need them for extra care are immediately granted the necessary time from their daily work. Although the kibbutz subscribes to the principle that it does more harm than good for parents to interfere too frequently with the nurses' work, the children's houses are, in practice, always open to parents.

There is no conclusive scientific evidence, to my knowledge, of the superiority of one family system over another. No all-embracing scientific study has been made of the kibbutz children. From a kibbutz point of view, what is known about the second and third kibbutz generations is decidedly encouraging. Most of the new generation have decided to remain in the kibbutz and in many cases have already taken over actual operation of the community. Less overtly intellectual, less prone to casuistic discussion than its parents, the second generation was for a long time a disappointment to its elders. The Israeli War of Independence, however, in which kibbutz children played a major role, established their position of leadership within the kibbutz movement. Many of those who were killed left a rich literature of memoirs, diaries, and other writings, much to the surprise of the elders who had not realized that their farm children were capable of this type of self-expression.

Educators both inside and outside the kibbutz agree that kibbutz children, as a result of the emphasis on modern educational techniques and the cultural environment in general, are more alert, sensitive, and talent-conscious than the average run of farm children elsewhere. They charge, however, that they are also overprotected and spoiled as a result of the very same factors.

Kibbutz children develop a feeling that the whole community revolves about them. They receive the best housing, the best food, and the best clothing, markedly superior to the quality of such services received by their parents. They are often oblivious to the financial difficulties in which the kibbutz many be involved. In Ramat Yohanan, for example, during my stay there, there were a number of instances of eighteen-year-olds revolting at graduating from the children's dining room to that of the adults. They turned up their noses at the quality of the food and service there. Though children are taught to clean their own quarters and to take care of their own needs, they nevertheless live secure in the knowledge that a housekeeper has been specifically assigned by the work program to clean up after them. The case of the kibbutz child who, when asked to clean up in the children's house, turns to the housekeeper and says, "But she's supposed to do it," is usual enough to be cited in many different kibbutzim by women who have been in such a housekeeping position. Disciplining is difficult. If parents are to see their children only for several hours during the day, it is only the strong parent who will risk embittering these few hours by denying the children's wishes or by disciplining them.

Despite these factors, however, kibbutz children turn out surprisingly independent and capable of coping with adult problems. Young children, for example, learn to feed themselves in kibbutzim at an earlier age than do children in private homes. They are not dependent on their parents and they learn to make their own decisions. They are at home in all kinds of social situations. They are good workers. Leadership potential is spotted and developed. Alertness to group developments and awareness of other people and their problems become second nature. Childhood is a happy experience and the loyalty to the kibbutz which is developed is not only loyalty to ideas but loyalty to a specific home of which the child feels an integral and accepted part. The child is familiar, too, with the inner workings of the country as a whole, having experienced, ever since he can remember, the intimate relationship between his parents and the kibbutz generally and Zionist and Israeli affairs.

American psychologists have studied the kibbutz children in comparison with non-kibbutz children in Israel. Part of their studies of ten-year-olds and seventeen-year-olds dealt with attitudes of children towards parents. They found that in the first place, despite the fact that the kibbutz children do not live "at home" with their parents and siblings as part of a tightly knit family unit, most of them showed positive attitudes towards their families. Such attitudes were clearly positive in more of the kibbutz children than in the non-kibbutz children. In addition, a kibbutz child tends to have a rather strong identification with his family and a tendency to feel that it is better than other families.

These trends are not outstanding, but at least the family unit appears to be a rather meaningful concept to the kibbutz child, though it does not exist as an economic unit or as the outstanding socializing agent in the life of the child. A similar trend shows up with respect to attitudes towards individual parents. Among the ten-year-olds in these studies, as many, and in some respects more, kibbutz children regard parents in a positive light than do non-kibbutz children. Perhaps the nurses and teachers, in carrying out most of the discipline and directing the socialization of the child, drain off to themselves whatever hostility and ambivalence arise in the children as a reaction to the frustrations of training. This explanation has also been suggested by other observers who have pointed out that the parents in the kibbutz, because of the limited time that they spend with their children, are very permissive and indulgent – like grandparents.

Related to the attitudes toward family and parents is the phenomenon of sibling rivalry which looms importantly in the atmosphere of the ordinary family. The limited information available points in the direction of rare occurrences of intense sibling rivalry among kibbutz children. From a very early age the kibbutz child is reared with a group of like-age but biologically unrelated "siblings." He knows of no life without these "siblings." He is used to having them around, having lived and shared with them from the very beginning of his existence. The experience of having to share, therefore, is less traumatic than with the child of an ordinary family when a new sibling "appears" on the scene. Among the kibbutz children, whatever rivalry may have been present in the peer unit in infancy has long been worked out in the daily interaction in which sharing and cooperating are positive dicta and principles. Some carryover of the resulting attitudes into the biological family is inevitable.

In the ordinary family, children usually identify strongly with the parent of their own sex. Boys imitate their fathers and want to be like them; girls want to be like their mothers. The parents are the nearest models and the closest ones emotionally. In the kibbutz, however, the situation is much more complex. There are several significant figures in the life of the child – the parent, the nurse, the teacher, and the peers. The nurse, teacher, and peers are frequently, and over longer periods of time, much nearer to the child than are the parents.

Kibbutz-reared adolescents (seventeen-year-olds) were compared in a number of dimensions with a group of non-kibbutz high school youngsters of the same age. The intellectual advantage of the kibbutz children seems to be maintained in adolescence. In written material, the kibbutz adolescents show greater range and complexity of ideas. They also show more interest in education and intellectual pursuits than do their peers of the ordinary farm families. Their interest in education and self-improvement seems in a way to compensate for the absence of long-range occupational goals.

Despite a great amount of evasiveness - common in the investigation of adolescents - the data on seventeen-year-olds also indicate the trend, shown among the ten-year-olds, regarding attitudes toward family and parental figures. The attitudes of the kibbutz adolescents are at least as frequently positive as - and in some instances more so than - those of the non-kibbutz adolescents. There do not seem to be any serious obstacles to the maintenance of such relationships and attitudes throughout the developmental period.

Another area on which some material emerged concerns sexuality. The kibbutz adolescent seems to reflect a much stricter, almost rigid, code with regard to sex than does the non-kibbutz adolescent. For the kibbutz seventeen-year-old having complete sex relations before marriage is unthinkable - "it would ruin one's life." He rejects the idea with greater scorn and finality, generally, than does the non-kibbutz boy or girl. Perhaps the close interaction between the sexes in the living quarters in the kibbutz, their continuous physical proximity, dictates the use of a more powerful regulation of sexual behavior.

It is also of great significance that the mother is not responsible for toilet training, and the parents in fact have little responsibility for training in general. This reduces the ambivalent tensions in the parent-child relationship to which we are accustomed in Western communities, since the mother is not the source of frustrations and the parents are not the chosen instruments of society for imposing its demands on the children. They are free to be only the good parents, except for the minority whose personal problems do not permit them to find satisfaction in this role. The advantages of this situation are seen in adolescence, when the relations between parents and children appear to be much less conflicting than we expect in Western communities and it probably also has something to do with the fact that the majority of kibbutz children were eager to continue the communal way of life and only a few tended to break away.

Kibbutz children are actually much closer to their parents in some ways than most North American children - if not to their parents as persons, then as members of the community. It is the kibbutz which is central to all learning, formal and informal, in the children's village. From the toddlers' school on, the children take daily hikes to visit their parents at work. At the machine shops, the barns, the olive groves, the children are stopped by adults, talked to, joked with, praised, perhaps asked to lend a hand. Thus the child is made to feel a welcome and important part of his father's and mother's occupational activities and those of the whole community – an experience which most North American children would probably envy. So, too, all big communal events in the kibbutz, such as holiday celebrations, are related to work that parents and children both have a part in, such as the festival of the first fruits, arbor day, or the harvest festival.

Something like two hundred or so kibbutzim care for their children in the manner I have described. In recent years, Gesher Haziv, a kibbutz that was founded largely by North American settlers, along with some other kibbutzim has adopted the system of having the children sleep in rooms adjoining those of their parents. Eight kibbutzim have adopted this new approach. For the past few years a group in Kfar Blum, another kibbutz, has agitated long and assiduously for the adoption of such a system. Its most vocal advocates were people from the United States. Thus, while there was some basis to the thought that the kibbutz was split along lines of national origin, the issue really cut across them.

The arguments for the change ran something like the following. It was alleged that it is more natural for the children to sleep near their parents. Then it was said that the night care of the children was hopelessly inadequate. There were many instances where a child had cried for a long time before the night watch attendant came to his aid. On psychological grounds it was argued that children between the ages of two and five were asocial creatures and needed to have a place where they could get away from their fellows. Instances of bed-wetting and thumb-sucking were cited as evidence of the insecurity of the children. It was suggested that the children could be watched more carefully by a mother who puts her children to bed at home than by one who puts them to bed in a children's house. Parents who have three or more children, it was pointed out, have to go to three or more different houses to put their children to bed. This involves quite a bit of physical exertion and discomfort, especially in the rainy season. Bedding the youngsters under one roof would make life easier. It was indicated that the children's houses, at bedtime, are often noisy, whereas quiet at this hour is desirable for growing children. Another allegation was that the new method would make the mother happier. These, in substance, were the arguments for the change.

The defenders of the *status quo* also had an arsenal of arguments. They felt, as do conservatives the world over, that an institution as widely accepted as the kibbutz system for sleeping of children must have intrinsic merit apart from the forces of inertia. They argued that the psychological argument was fallacious, inasmuch as the fundamental security or insecurity of the child was determined by the stability of the family unit, especially that of the parents; that while the present system might not be the best possible for the child at each stage of his development, it offered no insuperable emotional difficulties to the child rooted in a happy family. It was argued that if the children slept in the parents' quarters, the parents would have to stay home with the crying babies and would be prevented from attending meetings and social and cultural events. The allegation was made that the whole plan, as suggested, was nothing more than an elaborate rationalization to enable the individual to return to the familiar social and familial patterns that he had known in Europe. Further, the execution of such a plan at Kfar Blum would entail an investment of tens or hundreds of thousands of Israeli pounds, which the economy could ill afford. The final argument was that kibbutz children, grown under the existing system, had managed to develop into a generation of youth of whom one could be proud.

In my opinion, the kibbutz parents are richly rewarded. From all descriptions and from my own observations, the children turn into exceptionally courageous, self-reliant, secure, unneurotic, and deeply committed adults who find their self-realization in work and in marriage. They marry in their early twenties and soon have children who in turn are brought up in the communal nurseries and schools. There are almost no divorces and adultery is rare and severely censured. The marriages are not only stable but by North American standards exceptionally satisfactory; marriage is, in fact, the most important and intimate relationship of kibbutz adults.

The kibbutz-reared adults are genuinely fond of children, and this interest in children develops early. Young girls in kindergarten often assist their mothers who are nurses in younger children's houses; and girls in the grammar school frequently supervise the play of nursery children. Many of the high school girls also work in the various nurseries as afternoon relief nurses and, with rare exceptions, they are warm, loving, and intelligent workers. Later, as parents, they are warm and affectionate with their children, but relaxed and unanxious. Yet they have no desire to return to raising them privately at home. They are well satisfied with the way they themselves were communally reared. Not having experienced deep emotional attachment to parents as the core of their own development, and presently having a full life of their own, they do not feel they are missing anything by being parted from their children. Without doubt or hesitation parents place their new-born infants in the autonomous children's society.

It must be recalled that the kibbutz was formed during the pioneering days of the land of Israel, when the land had to be rebuilt out of swamps, deserts, and barren fields. It was a time of challenge, endurance, and human sacrifice. Those days called for new approaches to family living and so the kibbutz family was born. Today, when the State of Israel has emerged from the early founding days into a growing industrial urban society, the winds of change have slowly touched the lives of the kibbutz society. Within the next twenty-five years we may see a complete change in the kibbutz family system or an adaptation of the present family system.

A final thought about the family in the kibbutz is echoed at the close of Bruno Bettleheim's latest book, *The Children of the Dream:*

> The dreams parents dream for their children never come true – though neither are they wholly in vain. One cannot dream up a life for the other, one can only fashion a life of one's own. This the founders of the kibbutz have done, and it left its mark on their children. Perhaps it says something of kibbutz education that in some ways its children turned out as their parents expected and hoped, but in other respects very differently. These children of theirs are not the stuff dreams are made of, but real people, at home since their birth, on native ground.

PART 2

Annotated Bibliography

Bibliography

JEWISH LIFE: BACKGROUND SOURCES

Baron, Salo Wittmayer
A Social and Religious History of the Jews. Philadelphia: Jewish Publication Society of America, 1960. 8 vols.

The Index for Volumes I to VIII published in 1960 has references to marriage (p. 92) and family life (p. 49).

Berkovits, Eliezer, Horace M. Kallen, Abraham Menens, and **Levi Olan**
"Who is a Jew?: A Symposium," *Judaism,* VIII (Winter 1959), 3-15

Four men, each in his own way, try to answer the difficult question of "Who is a Jew?" They explore the historical, philosophical, societal, psychological, and purely religious aspects of the question and try to arrive at a definition that will be meaningful to everyone.

David, Jay, ed.
Growing Up Jewish. New York: William Morrow, 1969

Twenty-five selections deal with Jewish life from 1571 to the present day. Each author includes material on family life of his or her day.

Elbogen, Ismar
A Century of Jewish Life. Philadelphia: Jewish Publication Society of America, 1944

A historical overview of Jewish life in the early twentieth century in Europe, the Near East, and North America.

Epstein, Isidore
Judaism: A Historical Presentation. London: Penguin Books, 1959

The author discusses the development of religious and ethical teachings of Judaism. Marriage, mixed marriages, and divorce are included in his analysis.

Goldin, Hyman E.
The Jew and His Duties. New York: Hebrew Publishing, 1953

A guide to the observance of Judaism, the laws, commandments, rituals and prayers that govern every phase of Jewish life, including marriage and family. Written from an Orthodox Jewish point of view.

Heller, Abraham Major
The Vocabulary of Jewish Life. New York: Hebrew Publishing, 1942

Seven-hundred and fifty Judaic concepts constituting the major vocabulary of Jewish life, including the home, family, the calendar, ethics, values, etc., are contained in this book.

Kirshenbaum, David
Fast Days and Feast Days: Judaism Seen through Its Festivals. New York: Bloch Publishing, 1968

A Canadian Rabbi discusses the beauty, symbolism, and effect of Jewish festivals and fasts on Jewish life.

Millgram, Abraham E.
Sabbath, the Day of Delight. Philadelphia: Jewish Publication Society of America, 1965

As well as being a guide for Sabbath observance, this book seeks to make American Jewry aware of the importance of the Sabbath as an institution in the pattern of Jewish life.

Pearl, Chaim, and **Reuben S. Brookes**
A Guide to Jewish Knowledge. 4th ed. London: Jewish Chronicle Publications, 1965

A handbook of Jewish religion, geared to the religious student, which contains sections on religious observances, dietary laws, and sources of Jewish thought.

Reik, Theodor
Pagan Rites in Judaism. New York: Farrar, Straus and Giroux, 1964

Ten essays by a psychoanalyst explore the extent to which the pagan and prehistoric survive in the rites of Judaism as they are performed today. One essay deals with family solidarity (pp. 158-178).

Sperling, Abraham Isaac
Reasons for Jewish Customs and Traditions. Trans. by Abraham Matts. New York: Bloch Publishing, 1968

A compendium of Jewish ritual, customs, traditions, and ceremonials according to the Bible, Codes of Law, and other religious sources. Published in Hebrew originally in 1892.

Spiro, Saul S., and **Rena M. Spiro**
The Joy of Jewish Living. Cleveland: Bureau of Jewish Education, 1965

A junior-high school text about the Jewish way of life, its institutions, customs, ceremonies, and values.

Wirth, Louis
The Ghetto. Chicago: University of Chicago Press, 1956

A classic sociological study which analyzes the development of the Jewish ghetto from mediaeval times to the ghetto in metropolitan America.

Wouk, Herman
This is My God. New York: Dell Publishing, 1959

A portrait of the Jewish faith including its attitudes on the life cycle rituals, love and marriage, and death. The author is a well-known novelist, and himself a practicing Orthodox Jew.

HOME

Batist, Bessie W., ed.
A Treasure for My Daughter. New York: Hawthorn Books, 1968

Jewish holidays, ceremonies, benedictions, and other highlights of Jewish family life, as well as special menus for special occasions, are outlined in this guide.

Dresner, Samuel H., and **Seymour Siegel**
The Jewish Dietary Laws. New York: The Burning Bush Press, 1966

The meaning of the Jewish dietary laws, or *kashrut,* from which the term "keeping kosher" comes, is discussed in one essay. The second essay is a concise Jewish family guide to the observance of *kashrut.*

Goldin, Hyman E.
The Jewish Woman and Her Home. New York: Hebrew Publishing, 1941

A guide to Jewish family living from an Orthodox Jewish point of view. Includes regulations dealing with the home, festivals, and family life.

Goldman, Alex J.
A Handbook for the Jewish Family. New York: Bloch Publishing, 1958

A guide to Jewish holidays, the ways they are observed in the home, and the roles of the family members in the observances.

Goodman, Philip
The Passover Anthology. Philadelphia: The Jewish Publication Society of America, 1962

An account of the holiday of Passover which contains a historical section and a descriptive section covering the traditions and observances of the celebration in the home.

Greenberg, Betty D., and **Althea O. Silverman**
The Jewish Home Beautiful. New York: National Women's League of the United Synagogue of America, 1958

The customs, traditions, and ceremonies of the Jewish home throughout the years are set forth in this book which is offered to Jewish wives as a guide for Jewish homemaking.

Lang, Leon S.
"Jewish Family Living and the Sabbath," *Conservative Judaism,* VIII (June 1952), 1-17

The author discusses the psychological, traditional, and cultural role of the Sabbath in Jewish family life and suggests that Jews should reactivate the traditional ways of celebrating the Sabbath.

Levi, Shonie B., and **Sylvia R. Kaplan**
Guide for the Jewish Homemaker. New York: Schocken Books, 1964

A guide for homemaking for the Jewish family. Includes a large section on observing the Jewish holidays.

Perry, Mrs. Milton M.
"The Shabbat: A Family Affair," *Your Child,* II (Winter 1969), 18-20

Mrs. Perry recommends that Jews reinstate the consistent celebration of the Sabbath. She feels that this could be a binding family force, and recommends several ways in which it can be accomplished.

Rose, Evelyn
The Jewish Home. London: Valentine Mitchell, 1969

A comprehensive guide to the running of a Jewish household.

Rubens, Alfred
A History of Jewish Costume. London: Valentine Mitchell, 1967

The author traces developments of Jewish dress from more than four thousand years ago through many periods to the present day. He shows the significance of tradition and regional influences. The book contains over three hundred illustrations.

Segal, Samuel M.
The Sabbath Book. New York: Thomas Yoseloff, 1942

The author examines the rituals and family customs related to the Jewish sacred day, the Sabbath.

MARRIAGE

Brav, Stanley R., ed.
Marriage and the Jewish Tradition. New York: Philosophical Library, 1951

This collection of essays by a number of scholars, including Martin Buber, Leo Baeck, Felix Adler, and others, deals with traditional Jewish concepts of marriage, highlighting Jewish values and the historical framework of Jewish family life.

Breuer, Joseph
The Jewish Marriage: Source of Sanctity. New York: Philipp Feldheim, 1956

An Orthodox rabbi addresses this booklet to the about-to-be-married pair. He outlines some of the duties and obligations related to traditional Jewish marriage.

Drazin, Nathan
Marriage Made in Heaven. New York: Bloch Publishing, 1961

A guide book to marital relations by an Orthodox rabbi, who blends sexual behavior and religious customs.

Elman, Peter, ed.
Jewish Marriage. London and New York: Soncino Press, 1967

The specific Jewish type of family that has emerged from the peculiar history and traditions of the Jews is examined. The contributing authors geared this book to those about to marry, and they discuss some practical problems associated with contemporary family life.

Epstein, Lewin E.
The Ketuba: Jewish Marriage Contracts through the Ages. New York: Sabra Books, 1968

The Jewish marriage contract is a valuable source of information for students of economics and social history. This text is well illustrated.

Epstein, Louis M.
Marriage Laws in the Bible and the Talmud. Cambridge: Harvard University Press, 1942

A survey of Jewish law on the subject of marriage as it has developed historically from the beginning of existing records to the 1930s. The first three chapters examine polygamy, concubinage, and levirate marriages. The last three chapters cover the impediments to marriage, i.e., intermarriage, incest, and other marriage prohibitions.

Gittlesohn, Roland B.
My Beloved Is Mine: Judaism and Marriage. New York: Union of American Hebrew Congregations, 1969

Taking the Jewish religious traditions as the basis for discussion, the author examines love, marriage, and sexuality.

Gittlesohn, Roland B.
Consecrated unto Me: A Jewish View of Love and Marriage. New York: Union of America Hebrew Congregations, 1965

Primarily for use in religious schools, this book presents a Jewish view of marriage, focusing beyond the biological to the moral issues as well.

Goldstein, Sidney E.
Meaning of Marriage and Foundations of the Family: A Jewish Interpretation. New York: Bloch Publishing, 1940

In this booklet, a rabbi discusses the traditional Hebrew laws related to marriage and family development, and then examines Jewish family life today. Among the topics covered are birth control, intermarriage, divorce, and chastity and fidelity.

Goodman, Philip, and **Hanna Goodman**, eds.
The Jewish Marriage Anthology. Philadelphia: The Jewish Publication Society of America, 1965

This book portrays the spiritual pattern of Jewish marriage throughout the ages, and in many lands. Material is derived from the Bible, Talmud, and mediaeval Jewish literature.

Gordon, Albert I.
Bride and Groom: A Manual for Marriage. New York: The United Synagogue of America, 1959

A guide to those who plan to marry, explaining the religious meaning of the Jewish marriage ceremony and the rituals related to marriage.

Hollingshead, August B.
"Cultural Factors in the Selection of Marriage Mates," *American Sociological Review,* XV (October 1950), 619-627. Also in Robert F. Winch, and Robert McGinnis, eds. *Selected Studies in Marriage and the Family.* New York: Henry Holt, 1953, pp. 399-412

The author examines a body of data to determine how, and to what extent, specific factors influence the selection of marital partners. The data were taken from marriage licenses in New Haven in 1948. Ethnic origin is discussed among other factors.

Kahana, K.
The Theory of Marriage in Jewish Law. Leiden: E. J. Brill, 1966

This study of the theory on which Jewish laws concerning marriage are based is written for those who understand the Talmudic methods of discussion.

Lamm, Norman
A Hedge of Roses: Jewish Insights into Marriage and Married Life. New York: Philipp Feldheim, 1966

Some thoughts on Jewish marriage and the institutions associated with family life.

Lasker, Arnold A.
"The Rabbi and the Pre-Marital Interview," *Conservative Judaism,* VI (Winter 1949-1950), 20-33

Rabbis are urged to utilize the opportunity of the pre-marital interview for the purpose of guidance for the engaged couple.

Mace, David R.
Hebrew Marriage: A Sociological Study. London: Epworth Press, 1953

This study deals with the Old Testament teachings on sex, marriage, parenthood, and family life. The author also analyzes common difficulties in modern marriage.

"Marriage"
In *A Dictionary of the Bible.* Ed. by James Hastings. vol. III. New York: Charles Scribner and Sons, 1900, 262-278

A detailed account of the marriage procedures, forms, and duties, and the legal dissolution of marriage.

"Marriage"
In *The Interpreter's Dictionary of the Bible.* vol. III. New York: Abingdon Press, 1962, 278-287

The forms of biblical marriage are described and an analysis made of the marriage transaction.

"Marriage"
In *The Universal Jewish Encyclopedia.* Ed. by Isaac Landman. vol. III. New York: Universal Jewish Encyclopedia, Inc., 1942, 369-376

A detailed account of marriage in biblical times and in Rabbinical law. The material covers such items as impediments to marriage, marriage ceremony, obligations and rights of the couple, and property rights.

"Marriage, Marriage Ceremonies, and Marriage Laws"
In *Jewish Encyclopedia.* vol. VIII. New York: Funk and Wagnalls, 1925, 335-349

A detailed account of biblical marriage, Rabbinical literature related to marriage, marriage ceremonies around the world, and traditional marriage laws.

Max, Morris, and **Charles B. Ravel**
Marriage and Home: A Jewish Guide for Marital Happiness. New York: Rabbinical Council of America, 1959

In this booklet two Orthodox rabbis discuss the Jewish concept of marriage and the Jewish dietary laws.

Neufeld, E.
Ancient Hebrew Marriage Laws, with Special Reference to General Semitic Laws and Customs. London: Longmans, Green, 1944

A detailed survey of the marriage laws and customs among the ancient Hebrews as contained in the Old Testament. Includes a seven-page bibliography.

Rabinowicz, Harry
"The Shadchan," *The Jewish Spectator,* October 1961, pp. 14-16

The history of the "Shadchan," or matchmaker, in Jewish tradition is briefly traced. The author defines the role of the matchmaker, and elaborates on the needs it fulfilled. He also feels that some similar person might fulfil similar needs in the modern community.

Rabinowitz, Stanley
A Jewish View of Love and Marriage. Washington, D.C.: B'nai B'rith Youth Organization, 1961

Written as a guide to Jewish teen-agers, this booklet utilizes the Bible, Talmud, and various other Jewish traditional sources for commentary and advice on all the aspects of love and marriage. It deals with the validity and stability of love, the place of sex in pre-marital and marital relationships, the right time for marriage, etc.

Routtenberg, Lilly S., and **Ruth R. Seldin**
The Jewish Wedding Book. New York: Harper and Row, 1967

A guide to the traditions and social proprieties of the Jewish wedding, written by the wife and daughter of a well-known rabbi. The authors distinguish between Orthodox, Conservative, and Reform practices.

Shoulson, Abraham B., ed.
Marriage and Family Life: A Jewish View. New York: Twayne Publishers, 1959

In five sections, consisting of 30 different articles dealing with areas of human relationships in marriage, the contributors aim to interpret basic Jewish religious teachings in the light of the behavioral sciences.

INTERMARRIAGE

Barnett, Larry D.
"The Influence of Arguments Encouraging Interracial Dating," *Family Life Coordinator,* XII (July-October 1963), 91-92

A questionnaire administered to 212 Caucasian students at Oregon State University asked which arguments in favor of interracial dating they felt had most influence in encouraging it. Barnett's personal conclusion was that while youth payed lip service to the democratic heritage as a strong influence they seemed unwilling to exercise the freedom of experimentation that is basic to democracy.

Barnett, Larry D.
"Research in Interreligious Dating and Marriage," *Marriage and Family Living,* XXIV (May 1962), 191-194

Barnett points out that as interfaith dating and marriage are increasing, we must make an attempt to become aware of the problems that are involved. He summarizes the reasons for the increased rate, outlines the inherent special problems, and finally suggests how people can resolve some of the problems.

Berman, Louis A.
Jews and Intermarriage: A Study in Personality and Culture. New York: Thomas Yoseloff, 1968

A comprehensive review of social and psychological studies related to Jewish intermarriage. An extensive bibliography is included.

Besanceney, Paul H.
"On Reporting Rates of Intermarriage," *The American Journal of Sociology,* LXX (May 1965), 717-721

The author recommends that several points in methodology be implemented when reporting rates of intermarriage.

Bossard, James H. S., and **Eleanor Stoker Ball**
One Marriage - Two Faiths. Philadelphia: Ronald Press, 1957

Most of the difficulties likely to be found in interfaith marriages are discussed in this book.

Burchinal, Lee G.
"Membership Groups and Attitudes toward Cross-Religious Dating and Marriage," *Marriage and Family Living,* XXII (August 1960), 248-253

The effect of several variables on attitudes toward cross-religious dating and marriage was tested in this study conducted in rural and urban Iowa. Burchinal predicted that negative attitudes would be more prevalent among students with high religiosity, higher status, and those attending college, than among high school students and females generally. His hypotheses were generally supported by the findings, with an interesting variation concerning the sex variable.

Cahnman, Werner J. ed.
Intermarriage and Jewish Life. New York: Herzl Press, 1963

The thirteen papers in this book are the result of a symposium on intermarriage. In his introduction, Cahnman stresses the fact that intermarriage is on the increase, and that this is very much a problem facing North American Jewry.

Camazine, Ruth
"Intermarriage in the United States: A Review of the Literature," *The Jewish Social Work Forum,* IV (Spring 1967), 43-63

The reasons and motivations for intermarriage are considered in the literature reviewed here, with a view to helping Jewish communal workers deal effectively with this issue when it arises.

Christensen, Harold T., and **Kenneth E. Barber**
"Interfaith versus Intrafaith Marriage in Indiana," *Journal of Marriage and the Family,* XXIX (August 1967), 461-469

Interfaith and intrafaith marriages in Indiana are compared in terms of the following areas: number of civil as opposed to religious ceremonies, minority group membership, age, occupational status, residence in urban or rural areas, and divorce rates.

Davis, Moshe
"Mixed Marriage in Western Jewry: Historical Background to the Jewish Response," *Jewish Journal of Sociology,* X (December 1968), 177-220

A survey of mixed marriages among Western Jewry and a plea to re-examine present-day trends.

Eisenstein, Ira
Intermarriage. New York: The Burning Bush Press, 1964

This booklet, written by a rabbi, is representative of views held on intermarriage within the Conservative movement.

Ellman, Israel
"Jewish Intermarriage in the United States of America," *Dispersion and Unity,* No. 9 (1969), pp. 111-142

Reviews existing studies related to Jewish intermarriage in America.

Gendler, Everett
"Identity, Invisible Religion, and Intermarriage," *Response,* III (Winter 1969-70), 17-35

The author deals with questions related to intermarriage. He questions whether modern rabbis should participate in interfaith weddings.

Genné, William H.
How Mixed Can a Marriage Get? New York: Association Press, 1967

This small booklet geared tó men in the American Armed Services discusses in general terms interracial and interreligious marriages.

Goldstein, Sidney, and **Calvin Goldscheider**
"Social and Demographic Aspects of Jewish Intermarriages," *Social Problems,* XIII (Spring 1966), 386-399

This report found that the extent of Jewish intermarriage in Greater Providence, Rhode Island, was low, and it suggests reasons for this phenomenon, pointing out, however, that intermarriage is definitely on the rise.

Gordon, Albert I.
The Nature of Conversion. Boston: Beacon Press, 1967

A study of 45 men and women who changed their religion. The motivations for conversion are analyzed. Among the converts were Jews, Catholics, and Protestants.

Gordon, Albert I.
Intermarriage: Interfaith, Interracial, Interethnic. Boston: Beacon Press, 1964

A comprehensive study of intermarriage by an American rabbi who is also trained in social anthropology. The study includes in-depth interviews with 17 intermarried couples, and a survey of the attitudes of 5,000 American college students concerning intermarriage.

Gordon, Albert I.
"Intermarriage: A Personal View," *The Jewish Spectator,* November 1964, pp. 2-4

In this rather strong injunction against intermarriage, Rabbi Gordon presents some of the more serious problems connected with it. He feels that intermarriage does not promote universal brotherhood, which is one of the stronger arguments in support of it.

Gordon, Albert I.
"Negro-Jewish Marriages: Three Interviews," *Judaism,* XIII (Spring 1964), 164-181

Three tape-recorded interviews of interracial marriages involving one Jewish partner are reproduced in this article by a Reform rabbi, who subsequently included this material in his book *Intermarriage.*

Hathorn, Raban, William H. Genné, and **Mordecai L. Brill,** eds.
Marriage: An Interfaith Guide for All Couples. New York: Association Press, 1970

Described as "the first interfaith marriage guide for the ecumenical age." The five parts of this volume deal with building a marriage, being parents, the family in the community, and special problems in mixed marriages. Two pages of recommended readings are included.

Heer, David M.
"The Trend of Interfaith Marriages in Canada: 1922-1957," *American Sociological Review,* XXVII (April 1962), 245-250

Jewish intermarriage statistics are included in this study of interfaith marriages.

Heiss, Jerold S.
"Interfaith Marriage and Marital Outcome," *Marriage and Family Living,* XXIII (August 1961), 229-233

This study was designed to determine whether religion *per se* affects the outcome of mixed marriages, or whether a variety of other factors may be more relevant. Each of the three religions covered produced different findings in different areas.

Hurvitz, Nathan
"Sixteen Jews Who Intermarried," *Yivo Annual of Jewish Social Science,* XIII (1965), 153-178

A critique of a study by Maria H. Levinson and Daniel T. Levinson (*Yivo Annual of Jewish Social Science, XII*) about Jews who intermarried.

Kaplan, Joseph
"A Bibliography on Intermarriage," *In the Dispersion,* VII (July 1967), 172-178

A non-annotated bibliography of intermarriage involving Jews in North America and Europe, which contains about one hundred eighty items in English, German, Yiddish, and Italian.

Kirshenbaum, David
Mixed Marriages and the Jewish Future. New York, Bloch Publishing, 1958

An impressionistic view of a growing problem among Jewish families by an Orthodox Canadian rabbi.

Levinson, Maria H., and **Daniel J. Levinson**
"Jews Who Intermarry: Sociopsychological Basis of Ethnic Identity and Change," *Yivo Annual of Jewish Social Science,* XII (1958-1959), 103-130

A study of 16 couples whose marriage at the time of the study had lasted from six months to twelve years, most of them having been married from two to five years. Nine couples had children. Of the Jewish subjects, 11 were men, 5 women.

Mayer, John E.
Jewish-Gentile Courtships: An Exploratory Study of a Social Process. New York: The Free Press of Glencoe, 1961

The author identifies certain factors which lead Jews and gentiles into marriage with one another. His sample consisted of 45 couples, in 33 of which the husband was Jewish. The median ages at marriage were twenty-six for husbands and twenty-three for wives.

Mirsky, Norman
"Mixed Marriage and the Reform Rabbinate," *Midstream,* XVI (January 1970), 40-46

A discussion of the growing trend among a small group of Reform rabbis to perform mixed marriages without prior conversion of the non-Jewish spouse to Judaism.

Pike, James A.
If You Marry Outside Your Faith. New York: Harper and Brothers, 1954

Material on Christian-Jewish marriages is included in this guide to mixed marriages.

Prince, Alfred J.
"A Study of 194 Cross-Religious Marriages," *The Family Life Coordinator,* XI (January 1962), 3-7

The success of intermarriages, the areas of conflict in such marriages, how the couples solve their differences over religion, and which solutions seem to offer the best chance for success are all covered in this investigation.

Rodman, Hyman
"Technical Note on Two Rates of Mixed Marriage," *American Sociological Review,* XXX (October 1965), 776-778

Rodman deals with various ambiguous and conflicting methods of reporting data on mixed marriages. He suggests that a distinction always be made between mixed marriage rates *for marriage* and those *for individuals.* He also requests more accurate information on the source of the data, conversion rates, and clarification as to whether marriages discussed are first marriages or all marriages.

Rosenthal, Eric
"Studies of Jewish Intermarriage in the United States," *American Jewish Yearbook,* LXIV (1963), 3-53

The progress of assimilatory tendencies in the Jewish community is examined in a primarily rural State (Iowa) and a dense urban area (greater Washington, D.C.). The author discusses the implications of his findings for the growth of the Jewish community and for group cohesion.

Schlesinger, Benjamin
"Interfaith Marriages: Some Issues," *Social Science,* XLIII (October 1969), 217-221

A short review of the change evident in research related to Jewish intermarriage from 1930 to 1960.

Schlesinger, Benjamin
Bibliography on Interracial and Interreligious Marriage. Toronto: University of Toronto School of Social Work, 1968

A short 200-item bibliography on interracial and interreligious marriage covering Jewish and non-Jewish persons.

Schonfeld, Eugen
"Intermarriage and the Small Town: The Jewish Case," *Journal of Marriage and the Family,* XXXI (February 1969), 61-64

The contention that the exogamous Jew will lose his Jewish identity and dissociate himself from the Jewish community is examined and rejected in this study. The author has based his findings on observations in small towns where the rate of intermarriage is high.

Sklare, Marshall
"Intermarriage and Jewish Survival," *Commentary,* XLIX (March 1970), 51-58

A review of current studies of intermarriage and changes of attitude among the Reform rabbis.

Sklare, Marshall
"Intermarriage and the Jewish Future," *Commentary,* XXXVII (April 1964), 46-52

Sklare is concerned that the prevailing notions of the frequency of intermarriage are inaccurate and obsolete, and he defines what the new trend actually is. He discusses the phenomenon of intermarriage and what it will mean in the future to the American Jewish community.

Triebwasser, Marc A.
A Bibliography on Intermarriage. New York: Federation of Jewish Philanthropies, 1968

Nearly six hundred items, taken from popular and scientific literature, related to intermarriage of Jews in the United States are included in this non-annotated bibliography.

Zurofsky, Jack, ed.
The Psychological Implications of Intermarriage. New York: Federation of Jewish Philanthropies, 1966

The proceedings of a conference discuss intermarriage from a psychiatric, psychological, and social point of view. Four major papers and discussions are included in this book.

SEXUALITY

Borowitz, Eugene B.
Choosing a Sex Ethic: A Jewish Inquiry. New York: Schocken Books, 1969

A guide for personal conduct which examines four major ethics: healthy orgasm, mutual consent, love, and marriage. Nearly half of the book is devoted to notes related to material presented in the essays.

Dresner, Samuel H.
"Judaism and Sex," *Jewish Heritage,* X (Fall 1967), 48-50

A brief statement of the Jewish attitude toward sex taken from biblical sources.

Epstein, Louis M.
Sex Laws and Customs in Judaism. New York: Ktav Publishing House, 1967

A revision of the original book published by Dr. Epstein in 1948. It is a companion to his earlier work, *Marriage Laws in the Bible and the Talmud* (Harvard University Press, 1942), and deals with the Jewish code of sex conduct outside of marriage.

Feldman, David H.
Birth Control in Jewish Law. New York: New York University Press, 1968

A study which deals with marital relations, contraception, and abortion as set forth in the classic texts of Jewish law. The author interprets the legal and moral teachings of Judaism on such themes as sexual responsibility in marriage, the problems of irregular sex acts, and the historic and legal background of oral contraceptives.

Glasner, Samuel
"Judaism and Sex," in *The Encyclopedia of Sexual Behavior.* Ed. by Albert Ellis, and Albert Abarbanel. vol. II. New York: Hawthorn Books, 1964, 575-584

Rabbi Glasner cites authorities, Talmudic and biblical, to show that attitudes from the most free to the most inhibited are supported by some Jewish writings. The article suggests, however, that attitudes towards sex among Jews generally are moderate ones of fairly rational and ethical self-control.

Gordis, Robert
Sex and the Family in the Jewish Tradition. New York: Burning Bush Press, 1967

To gauge and understand the current revolution in morals and standards of conduct, the author returns to the Jewish tradition in laws and customs in dealing with morality, birth control, marital and extra-marital relations, divorce, and women's rights.

Gordis, Robert
"Marriage, Birth Control, Divorce," *Jewish Heritage,* X (Fall 1967), 42-47

A short summary of the author's booklet, *Sex and the Family in the Jewish Tradition.*

Kligfeld, Bernard
"Jewish Sex Ideals," *Sexology,* XXX (July 1964), 819-821

A rabbi discusses the sexual code of Judaism from biblical times to the present.

Patai, Raphael
Sex and Family in the Bible and the Middle East. New York: Doubleday Dolphin Books, 1959

An anthropological analysis of Middle-Eastern sexual customs which deals with the attitudes toward romantic love, incest, marriage, adultery, family life, and the position of women in the society of biblical times.

Piper, Otto A.
The Biblical View of Sex and Marriage. New York: Charles Scribner and Sons, 1962

The author discusses the nature of sex, children, sexual knowledge, the standards of sexual life, virtues of marriage, the problems of sexual relationship related to the Old and New Testaments. A five-page bibliography is included.

Spector, Samuel
"The Talmud on Sex," *The Jewish Spectator,* February 1969, pp. 19-22

Spector cites several quotations and opinions from the Talmud concerning various aspects of sex to support his contention that the Talmud treats sex realistically, and with some modernity.

HEALTH AND WELFARE

Bunim, Sarah
"Culture and Its Psychological Implication in Casework with the Jewish Client," *The Jewish Social Work Forum,* V (Fall 1968), 19-33

The writer has culled from casework material the particular aspects which emphasize the effects of Jewish cultural experience on the Jewish client.

Conrad, Gertrude
"Casework with Survivors of Nazi Persecution: Twenty Years after Liberation," *Journal of Jewish Communal Service,* XLVI (Winter 1969), 170-175

A general overview of the problems faced by the survivors of Nazi concentration camps, twenty years after their liberation from these camps.

Davids, Leo
"Honor Thy Foster Father: Some Jewish Thoughts," *The Jewish Social Work Forum,* VI (Spring 1969), 25-30

A discussion of Jewish foster fathers, and the Jewish attitude toward them.

Goldman, M.
"Characteristics of the Jewish Poor Served in a Family Agency: A Case Study," *Journal of Jewish Communal Service,* XLIII (March 1967), 249-252

A review of three different types of poor Jewish families in Baltimore and their characteristics.

Goldstein, Louis
"The Kinship System and Social Work Practice," *Journal of Jewish Communal Service,* XLIII (Fall 1966), 84-92

An article about many kinship systems and their relationship to social work practice, including some information on the Jewish system.

Graham, Saxon, *et al.*
"Religion and Ethnicity in Leukemia," *American Journal of Public Health,* LX (February 1970), 266-274

Among the 319 child patients under the age of fifteen years and the 1,414 adults examined were 84 Jewish patients. Religious background indicated no difference among the children, but among the adult cases, Jews had a higher risk factor than other ethnic groups under study.

Greifer, Julian L.
"The Family and the Jewish Community Center," *Journal of Jewish Communal Service,* XXXIV (Fall 1957), 98-108

A report on the growing amount of family disorganization and the role of the community center in helping improve the situation.

Horowitz, Isadore, and **Philip E. Enterline**
"Lung Cancer among the Jews," *American Journal of Public Health,* LX (February 1970), 275-282

A study of patterns of mortality from lung cancer among male and female Jews in Montreal.

Isenstadt, Theodore R.
"The Role of the Family Agency in the Jewish Community," *Jewish Social Service Quarterly,* XXXI (December 1954), 208-212

Some of the philosophical and professional questions concerning the functions and services of the family agency in the Jewish community are reviewed here.

Jakobovits, Immanuel
Jewish Medical Ethics. New York: Philosophical Library, 1959

The influence of Jewish religious laws on the activity and practice of the physician and his clients is explored in this volume.

Joffe, Stella
"Changes in Jewish Families Served by the Social Agency." *Journal of Jewish Communal Service,* XLV (Spring 1969), 232-235

An outline of five types of Jewish problem families requiring social agency help.

Jung, Leo
Human Relations in Jewish Law. New York: Jewish Education Committee Press, 1967

Rabbi Jung's aim is to describe the traditional sources from which Jewish communal services derived their inspiration through many centuries of Jewish community life.

Kertzer, Morris N., ed.
The Rabbi and the Jewish Social Worker. New York: Federation of Jewish Philanthropies, 1962

Twenty-six selections discuss the issues of Judaism and mental health, the role of the aged in Jewish life, adoption, and charity in Jewish thought and action.

Kutzik, Alfred T.
Social Work and Jewish Values. Washington, D.C.: Public Affairs Publishing, 1959

Discusses Jewish values in social work, including those which form the bases for some of the agencies set up by the Jewish communities.

Leichter, Hope Jensen, and **William E. Mitchell**
"Jewish Extended Familism," in Robert F. Winch, and Louis Wolf Goodman, eds. *Selected Studies in Marriage and the Family.* 3rd ed. New York: Holt, Rinehart and Winston, 1968, pp. 139-148

Some highlights of the findings of a study of Jewish families active with the Jewish Family Service of New York.

Leichter, Hope Jensen, and **William E. Mitchell**
Kinship and Casework. New York: Russell Sage Foundation, 1967

A study, conducted at the Jewish Family Service of New York, of 298 Jewish families and their kinship relations.

Lerner, Samuel
"The Meaning of Jewishness to Clients and Its Effect on Case Work Service," *Jewish Social Service Quarterly,* XXVII (June 1951), 371-381

A discussion, with case illustrations, of the reasons why clients come to Jewish agencies.

Lev, Aryeh
"Services to the Jewish Personnel in the Armed Forces and to Hospitalized Veterans," *Journal of Jewish Communal Service,* XLVI (Spring 1970), 228-237

There are approximately 5,000 Jewish patients in Veterans Hospitals, 200 in the Public Health Service Hospital, and 250 in St. Elizabeth's Hospital in the United States. Jews constitute 3 percent of America's Armed Forces.

Linzer, Norman
The Jewish Family. New York: Federation of Jewish Philanthropies, 1968

This compendium is designed to furnish basic information from Jewish sources on Jewish family life to social workers in Jewish agencies. The author covers such topics as abortion, adoption, the aged, birth control, death, divorce, intermarriage, parent-child relationships, etc.

Linzer, Norman
"Halachic Implications of Illegitimacy and Adoption for Social Work Practice," *The Jewish Social Work Forum,* IV (Spring 1967), 11-26

In the last decade, illegitimacy has been rising in the general population and in the Jewish community as well. This paper is concerned with the Halachic (Jewish law) perspective of the problem as well as the patterns and causes of it, and briefly traces the Halachic approach to illegitimacy and adoption and its implications for Jewish social workers.

Morris, Robert, and **Michael Freund,** eds.
Trends and Issues in Jewish Social Welfare in the United States, 1899-1958. Philadelphia: Jewish Publication Society, 1966

A history of American Jewish social welfare including the development of services for individuals and families.

Rogers, Candace L., and **Hope J. Leichter**
"Laterality and Conflict in Kinship Ties," in William J. Goode, ed. *Readings on the Family and Society.* Englewood Cliffs: Prentice-Hall, 1964, pp. 213-218

A short description of the kinship laterality of 147 Jewish families who were clients of a Jewish family agency in New York.

Rubin, Burton
"What's Jewish about Jewish Family Services?," *The Jewish Social Work Forum,* VI (Spring 1969), 17-24

Rubin points out that in Europe every small village had its charitable and philanthropic organization to look after its Jewish needy. The tradition of these organizations underlies and gives special meaning to the Jewish social service agencies today, and has much to do with the "special" character of the relationship of these organizations to their communities.

Teicher, Morton
"How Should Jewish Communal Agencies Relate to the Jewish Family Now and in the Future?," *Journal of Jewish Communal Service,* XLIV (June 1968), 320-329

The article contains a summary of the American Jewish family today, and recommendations for the future role of Jewish communal agencies in Jewish family life.

Tendler, Moshe D., ed.
A Hospital Compendium: A Guide to Jewish Moral and Religious Principles in Hospital Practice. New York: Federation of Jewish Philanthropies, 1969

This guide was developed to help the hospital staff appreciate the Jewish medical-ethical-religious values related to the Jewish patient and his care. Included is material on the value of life, death, sickness, dietary laws, holidays, autopsies, abortion, contraception, circumcision, and varied medical procedures.

Warach, Bernard
"Supporting and Enhancing Family Life through the Jewish Community Center," *Journal of Jewish Communal Service,* XLV (Summer 1969), 335-348

A review of the shortcomings in Jewish family life, and the remedies that the Jewish community center does, or can, provide.

Wechsler, Henry, Denise Horn, Harold W. Demone, Jr., and **Elizabeth H. Kasey**
"Religious Ethnic Differences in Alcohol Consumption," *Journal of Health and Social Behavior,* II (March 1970), 21-29

Data were collected on 8,461 patients admitted to hospital emergency service. The proportion of patients with positive indication of alcohol was lowest among Jewish persons and Italian Catholics.

Weiner, Milton
"Helping the Middle-Class Delinquents to Use Casework Service," *Journal of Jewish Communal Service,* XXXVIII (Spring 1962), 290-296

A review of middle-class delinquents in general, with some specific reference to problems of helping the middle-class Jewish delinquent and his family.

Weiss, Charles
"Circumcision in Infancy: A New Look at an Old Operation," *Clinical Pediatrics,* III (September 1964), 560-563

A discussion of the value of circumcision among Jewish children.

Weiss, Charles
"Ritual Circumcision: Comments on Current Practices in American Hospitals," *Clinical Pediatrics,* I (October 1962), 65-72

An examination of ritual circumcision among Jews in the United States.

Zaret, Melvin S.
"The Scope of the Jewish Family Agency," *Jewish Social Science Quarterly,* XXVIII (June 1952), 359-365

A review of the objectives and functions of a Jewish family agency.

Zborowski, Mark
People in Pain. San Francisco: Jossey Bass, 1969

Zborowski's study of Jewish, Italian, Irish, and Old American patients of a Veterans Hospital in New York, by revealing the differences among the four groups and the similarities between each group, supports his hypothesis that along with the major role which pathology might play in influencing a patient's response to his pain experience, the cultural background appears to be a most important, if not determining, factor in shaping behavior in pain and illness.

Zborowski, Mark
"Cultural Components in Responses to Pain," *Journal of Social Issues,* VIII (1952), 16-30

A comparative study of Jewish, Italian, Irish, and "Old American" patients in a Veterans Hospital in New York. The author examined their reactions to pain, and traces their feelings to family life in the formative years.

DEATH AND MOURNING

Gordon, Albert I.
In Times of Sorrow: A Manual for Mourners. New York: The United Synagogue of America, 1965

The rites and rituals of mourning related to the death of Jewish persons are outlined in this booklet.

Grollman, Earl A.
"The Ritualistic and Theological Approach of the Jew to Death," in Earl A. Grollman, ed. *Explaining Death to Children.* Boston: Beacon Press, 1967, pp. 223-245

A Rabbi analyzes Jewish religious customs, including mourning, around the death of a family member.

Lamm, Maurice
The Jewish Way in Death and Mourning. New York: Jonathan David, 1969

The Orthodox point of view of man's behavior as he confronts death and mourning is expressed by a rabbi. The various symbols and ceremonies around death are described.

Spiro, Jack D.
A Time to Mourn. New York: Bloch Publishing, 1967

A consideration, by a Reform rabbi, of the dynamics of the process of mourning, as revealed in modern psychiatric research, as well as the Jewish theological background relating to death, the hereafter, the soul, burial.

DIVORCE

Amram, David Werner
The Jewish Law of Divorce According to the Bible and the Talmud. 2nd ed. New York: Herman Press, 1968

A comparison of the biblical Talmudic view with that of the New Testament and Mohammedan Law. Some of the topics covered are forbidden marriages, the divorced woman and her rights, and the *get* (the Jewish divorce procedure).

Fried, Jacob, ed.
Jews and Divorce. New York: Ktav Publishing, 1968

These are papers of a conference called to examine what is happening to the Jewish family of today and the incidence of the rising divorce rate.

Grollman, Earl A.
"A Rabbi's View on Children of Divorce," in Earl A. Grollman, ed. *Explaining Divorce to Children.* Boston: Beacon Press, 1969, pp. 201-232

A rabbi discusses the Jewish attitude toward marriage and divorce, and the rules pertaining to custody of children.

Levin, Marlin
"Divorce: Israel Style," *Hadassah Magazine,* March 1969, pp. 13, 35-36

A review of the traditional view of divorce and remarriage according to religious law, and the present situation as it affects modern Israelis.

Sigal, Phillip
"The Rabbis and Divorce," *The Jewish Spectator,* October 1961, pp. 19-22

Rabbi Sigal is concerned that few Jews who become divorced nowadays go through the procedures of Jewish divorce laws. He reviews these laws and the reasons for their evolution, and suggests several ways in which they would be helpful to members of the modern community.

Whartman, Eliezer
"Divorce - Israel Style," *The Jewish Standard,* March 1966, pp. 5, 11-13

One of every ten marriages in Israel falls apart within the first year of marriage, and the majority of divorces take place between the tenth and fourteenth years. This article is based mostly on another article, taken from an Israeli newspaper, which discusses case histories of three divorces and some aspects of Israeli divorce law.

FAMILY LIFE: OVERVIEW

Bellman, Samuel Irving
"The Jewish Mother Syndrome," *Congress Bi-Weekly,* December 27, 1965

Bellman describes the symptoms of the "Jewish mother syndrome" and differentiates the Jewish mother from those of other cultures. He suggests, though, that the Jewish mother be evaluated positively as well for her role as a preserver of family strength and unity.

Blackman, Philip, ed.
Mishnayoth: Order Nashim. vol. III. New York: Judaica Press, 1965

This volume of the "Mishnah" deals with betrothal, marriage, divorce, and the relation of woman to man, and treats such matters as vows, the faithless wife, and intermarriage.

Boroff, David
"The Overprotective Jewish Mother," *Congress Bi-Weekly,* November 4, 1957, pp. 6-8

Boroff offers many of the standard explanations for the tendency of the Jewish mother to be overprotective, and elaborates on some of the consequences this form of "tyranny" may have for the other members of the family.

Duckat, Walter
"The Attitudes toward the Aged in Rabbinic Literature," *The Jewish Social Service Quarterly,* XXIX (Spring 1953), 320-324

A short review of opinions from Rabbinic literature regarding the place of the aged in Jewish life.

Fishman, Joshua
The Jewish Family. New York: Anti-Defamation League of B'nai B'rith, 1960

In this booklet a rabbi discusses some important changes in Jewish family life, indicating how distinctive traditional values have modulated these changes. This is an attempt to clarify both the differences and similarities between Christian and Jewish American family life.

Franzblau, Abraham
"A New Look at the Psychodynamics of Jewish Family Living," *Journal of Jewish Communal Service,* XXXV (Fall 1958), 57-71

A comparison of contemporary Jewish family life with family practices from biblical writings.

Ganzfried, Solomon, and **Hyman E. Goldin**
Code of Jewish Law. New York: Hebrew Publishing, 1961. 4 vols.

Volume IV of the code of Jewish Law contains matter related to marriage, sexuality, childbirth, family rituals, and child rearing. These volumes are the abridged "Shulhan Aruh" (code of law) originally compiled by Joseph ben Ephraim Caro (1488-1575), further annotated by Mosca ben Yisrael Isserles (1520-1572) and abridged by Rabbi Solomon Ganzfried in 1870.

Glatzer, Nahum
"The Jewish Family and Humanistic Values," *Journal of Jewish Communal Service,* XXXVI (Summer 1960), 269-273

A paper about the nature of the classical and contemporary Jewish family, as well as the possible future Jewish family in American society.

Glustrom, Simon
When Your Child Asks: A Handbook for Jewish Parents. New York: Bloch Publishing, 1956

A guide for Jewish parents on major issues of Jewish religious and social life.

Hertz, J. H., ed.
"On Marriage, Divorce, and the Position of Women in Judaism," in *Deuteronomy.* London: Oxford University Press, 1951, 310-321

In the discussion of Volume 5 of the Pentateuch or "Five Books of Moses," the editor reviews the biblical implications of marriage, divorce, and the role of women.

Isenstadt, Theodore R.
"Changing Social Orientation of the Jewish Aged: A Profile," *Journal of Jewish Communal Service,* XLI (Fall 1964), 124-131

Increasingly the trend is for older people to live in the community rather than in institutions, according to the author. He outlines ways in which Jewish community services and organizations might adapt to and help in this situation.

Kaplan, Benjamin
The Jew and His Family. Baton Rouge: Louisiana State University Press, 1967

The author integrates his own personal experiences, personal insight, and sociological findings to examine the Jewish family from biblical days to modern times.

Kitov, A. E.
The Jew and His Home. New York: Shengold Publishers, 1963

A contemporary restatement, by an Israeli author, of classic Jewish traditions dealing with marriage, the home, the role of the wife, and the family in modern society.

Landau, Sol
"The Jewish Interpretation of Love," *The National Jewish Monthly,* December 1961, pp. 6-7

Rabbi Landau describes the Jewish interpretation of love as an all-encompassing, ever-renewing, strength-giving union, with the integrity of the individual preserved in the relationship. He stresses that this is "real" love and demands work and patience. Therefore he recommends that the synagogues offer guidance and counseling by clergy and professionals to their young members.

Lang, Leon S.
"Jewish Values in Family Life," *Conservative Judaism,* I (June 1945), 9-18

In the author's opinion, Jewish family life is languishing almost to the point of extinction. He recommends that in order to combat this, Jewish leaders, teachers, and parents participate in a "renascence" of Jewish values in family living.

Lenski, Gerhard
The Religious Factor: A Sociologist's Inquiry. New York: Doubleday Anchor Books, 1963

Chapter V reviews the various factors related to family life and religion and the influence of religion in the family cycle.

Levine, Sidney
"Some Jewish Guidelines for Strengthening Family Life: A Proposal," *Jewish Social Work Forum,* IV (Spring 1967), 27-42

From his own experience the author has compiled ideas on social values in Jewish religion, culture, and psychology, and has formulated guidelines for caseworkers and therapists to help members of the Jewish community deal with such problems as marriage, intermarriage, sex, and child rearing.

Markowitz, S. H.
Leading a Jewish Life in the Modern World. New York: Union of American Hebrew Congregations, 1942

A Reform rabbi discusses parent-child relationships and Jewish home life.

Shapiro, Manheim
"The Jewish Heritage: What Is Woman's Place?," *Council Woman* (June 1967). A reprint. 4 pp.

The positive change in the status of the Jewish woman – in her role as wife and mother and daughter – is sketched here through the Bible to the present day. Shapiro postulates that modern woman may be better equipped to define her present-day feminine role by examining her Jewish heritage.

Shapiro, Manheim
"Jewish Family Values: Are They Breaking Down or Shifting?," *Council Woman* (February 1965). A reprint. 4 pp.

The author addresses himself to the possible breakdown of Jewish family values in terms of the Jewish divorce rate and delinquency rate. He then expresses his opinion about possible ways to revive "the solidarity, strength and ethic we associate with the classic Jewish family."

Shapiro, Manheim
"'In My Footsteps': Some Dilemmas of Jewish Parents," *Council Woman* (December 1963). A reprint. 4 pp.

Manheim provides his personal answers to the questions of many Jewish parents regarding the Jewish identity and education of their children.

Wolfenstein, Martha
"Two Types of Jewish Mothers," in Margaret Mead, and Martha Wolfenstein, eds. *Childhood in Contemporary Cultures.* Chicago: University of Chicago Press, 1955, pp. 424-440

A picture of two Jewish mothers, one of East European background, the other American-born. The mother-child relations are analyzed.

FAMILY LIFE IN BIBLICAL TIMES

Bardis, Panos D.
"Main Features of the Ancient Hebrew Family," *Social Science,* XXXVIII (June 1963), 168-183

An examination of engagement, the dowry, marriage, women, children, and divorce, related to the Hebrew family of the Old Testament.

Cross, Earle Bennett
"The Hebrew Family in Biblical Times," in Jeffrey K. Hadden, and Marie L. Borgotta, eds. *Marriage and the Family: A Comprehensive Reader.* Itasca: Ill.: F. E. Peacock Publishers, 1969, pp. 60-73

A review of the biblical teachings about marriage, endogamy, exogamy, the household, dissolution of marriage, the levirate, and the relations of parents and children.

Cross, Earle Bennett
The Hebrew Family: A Study in Historical Sociology. Chicago: University of Chicago Press, 1927

A study of the Hebrew family as it appears in the Old Testament.

Deen, Edith
Family Living in the Bible. New York: Harper and Row, 1963

The author expanded her master's thesis to present a popular approach to the topic of the family in the Bible. Her chapters include material on marriage; husband-wife relationships; the role of father, mother, and children; family breakdown; family concerns; and family strengths. After discussing the Hebrew family, she discusses aspects of the family related to the teachings of Jesus.

"Family"
In *A Dictionary of the Bible.* vol. I. Ed. by James Hastings. New York: Charles Scribner and Sons, 1900, 846-850

A short examination of the biblical family including the varied kinship patterns (siblings, husbands and wives, concubines).

"Family and Family Life"
In *Jewish Encyclopedia.* vol. V. New York: Funk and Wagnalls, 1925, 336-338

A short account of biblical aspects of Jewish family life.

Porter, Joshua Roy
The Extended Family in the Old Testament. London: Edutext Publications, 1967

In this essay, a Protestant scholar of the Old Testament discusses the obscure references contained in the Pentateuch to the extended family of ancient Israel.

Queen, Stuart A., and **Robert W. Habenstein**
"The Patriarchal Family of the Ancient Hebrews," in Queen and Habenstein, eds. *The Family in Various Cultures.* New York: J. B. Lippincott, 1965, pp. 138-158

A summary of findings related to the Ancient Hebrew family.

FAMILY LIFE IN THE MIDDLE AGES

Abrahams, Israel
Jewish Life in the Middle Ages. New York: Meridian Books, 1958

Chapters VII and VIII deal with monogamy and the home, Chapter IX with love and courtship, and Chapter X with marriage customs.

Falk, Z. W.
Jewish Matrimonial Law in the Middle Ages. London: Oxford University Press, 1966

Modern society is experiencing constant changes in marital relations and in the laws related to marriage. The author investigates similar changes in the development of the Jewish tradition within mediaeval Europe. He deals with monogamy, the forms of engagement and nuptials, divorce, and the status of married women.

Katz, Jacob
Tradition and Crisis: Jewish Society at the End of the Middle Ages. New York: The Free Press, 1961

This book appeared in the Hebrew original in 1958. It includes material on the family, kinship, and social life during the Middle Ages.

FAMILY LIFE IN EASTERN EUROPE

Ain, Abraham
"Swislocz: Portrait of a Jewish Community in Eastern Europe," *Yivo Annual of Jewish Social Science*, IV (1949), 86-114

In 1906 the town of Swislocz (Sislevich – Yiddish name) had 600 families, of whom 400 were Jewish. The author details life in this "shtetl," including socio-economic, social, and cultural activities.

Davidowicz, Lucy, ed.
The Golden Tradition: Jewish Life and Thought in Eastern Europe. Boston: Beacon Press, 1967

Fifty-seven selections cover the educational, social, political, and cultural aspects of Jewish life in Eastern Europe from 1830 to 1914.

Glicksman, William M.
In the Mirror of Literature. New York: Living Books, 1966

An analysis of the life of Jews in Poland, with emphasis on the economic patterns related to the Jewish community. The content gives insight into the ways in which families earned a living during the 1914-1939 period.

Landes, Ruth, and **Mark Zborowski**
"The Context of Marriage: Family Life as a Field of Emotions," in H. Kent Geiger, ed. *Comparative Perspectives on Marriage and the Family.* Boston: Little, Brown, 1968, pp. 77-102. Also in *Psychiatry,* XIII (1950), 447-464

The authors discuss various hypotheses about the form and functioning of the Jewish family in the now destroyed Eastern European small town known in Yiddish as the "shtetl."

Schlesinger, Benjamin
"The Vanished Shtetl," *The Jewish Standard,* April 1962, pp. 10, 83-89

The shtetl, the small town in Eastern Europe, was a unique way of life adapted to meet the peculiar needs of the Jew in Eastern Europe which was carried over to North America by European immigrants. This article deals primarily with the impact of the shtetl life-style on the family constellation in America.

Shtern, Yekhiel
"A Kheyder in Tishevits," *Yivo Annual of Jewish Social Science,* V (1950), 152-171

A "kheyder" was the Jewish elementary school in Eastern Europe prior to World War II. The author discusses in detail the life of the pupils in this school, and analyzes the educational methods used.

Zborowski, Mark
"The Place of Book-Learning in Traditional Jewish Culture," in Margaret Mead, and Martha Wolfenstein eds. *Childhood in Contemporary Cultures.* Chicago: University of Chicago Press, 1955, pp. 118-141. Also in *Harvard Educational Review,* XIX (Spring 1949), 87-109

The values and patterns related to education of Jewish children in the Eastern European shtetl (small town) are examined.

Zborowski, Mark, and **Elizabeth Herzog**
Life Is with People. New York: International Universities Press, 1955

This monograph is a primary source on Eastern European Jewish culture, from anthropological sources, first-hand observations, and first-person reports. Family life in the "shtetl" (small town) before World War I is described in detail.

FAMILY LIFE IN WESTERN EUROPE

Krausz, Ernest
"The Edgware Survey: Factors in Jewish Identification," *The Jewish Journal of Sociology,* XI (December 1969), 151-163

Includes a section on the influence of close kinship ties and child upbringing on Jewish identification in a community in England.

Krausz, Ernest
"The Edgware Survey: Occupation and Social Class," *The Jewish Journal of Sociology,* XI (June 1969), 75-95

Includes a section on the influence of the socio-economic position of parents on their children.

Krausz, Ernest
"The Edgware Survey: Demographic Results," *The Jewish Journal of Sociology,* X (June 1968), 83-100

A study of the demographic characteristics of the Jews in Edgware, England.

Oelener, Toni
"Three Jewish Families in Modern Germany," *Jewish Social Studies,* IV (July and October 1942), 241-268, 349-398

Study of the changes in the economic and social structure of three families after emancipation of the German Jews in the nineteenth century.

West, Vera
"The Influence of Parental Background on Jewish University Students," *The Jewish Journal of Sociology,* X (December 1968), 267-280

A study relating the religious position and observance of his parents to the stand of the English Jewish university student.

FAMILY LIFE IN THE U.S.A.

Community

Antonovsky, Aaron
"Aspects of New Haven Jewry: A Sociological Study," *Yivo Annual of Jewish Social Science,* X (1955), 128-164

The paper discusses the socio-economic data on a middle-sized Jewish community and Jewish identity of the Jews.

Brotz, Howard M.
The Black Jews of Harlem. New York: Schocken Books, 1970

A historical analysis of the black Jews of Harlem and their customs.

Edidin, Ben M.
Jewish Community Life in America. New York: Hebrew Publishing, 1947

This description of Jewish group life in the United States also covers Jewish social agencies, institutions, and organizations.

Fried, Jacob, ed.
Judaism and the Community. New York: Thomas Yoseloff, 1968

A compilation of articles which deal with some of the social problems faced by the Jew and his family. They include intermarriage, philanthropy, social welfare, and community relations.

Gans, Herbert
The Levittowners. New York: Pantheon Books, 1967

This is a sociological study of a suburb in New Jersey, where the author lived and observed for two years, studying how a new community comes into being, how people react to the suburbs, and, in general, the life and politics of the community.

Geller, Victor B.
"How Jewish is Jewish Suburbia," *Tradition,* II (Spring 1960), 318-330

The effect on Jewish life of the large movement of Jewish families to suburbia in America is discussed.

Ginzberg, Eli
"The Agenda Reconsidered," *Journal of Jewish Communal Service,* XLII (Spring 1966), 247-282

A revision and updating of a "blueprint" for the American Jewish community drawn by the author in 1949. Ginzberg discusses the goals and functions of communal services and organizations in terms of new cultural, societal, and economic factors such as the emergence of Israel, less anti-Semitism, Jewish youth's lack of concern about their past, and his feelings that there is an "erosion" of Jewish religious life.

Glazer, Nathan, and **Patrick Moynihan**
Beyond the Melting Pot. Cambridge: Harvard University Press, 1963

An examination of Negroes, Puerto Ricans, Jews (pp. 137-180), Italians, and Irish in New York City in the early twentieth century. The life of each group is described, including family patterns.

Goldberg, N.
"Jews in the Police Records of Los Angeles: 1933-1947," *Yivo Annual of Jewish Social Science,* V (1950), 266-291

A statistical analysis of police records which indicates that Jews have a lower police arrest rate than the general population.

Goldstein, Sidney, and **Calvin Goldscheider**
Jewish Americans: Three Generations in a Jewish Community. Englewood Cliffs: Prentice-Hall, 1968

Three main themes are pursued in this research study which deals with the changes in the sociological and demographical parameters of the Jewish community of Greater Providence, Rhode Island: the degree and form of change by the generations; differences between Jew and non-Jew; and Jewish heterogeneity. The general areas of inquiry include population structure, socio-economic status, family structure, and intermarriage.

Goodman, Philip, ed.
Dimensions and Horizons for Jewish Life in America. New York: National Jewish Welfare Board, 1966

A reader and guide, which includes various family topics.

Gordon, Albert I.
Jews in Suburbia. Boston: Beacon Press, 1959

A questionnaire sent to 89 communities located in ten States in the United States, as well as personal interviews with selected community leaders and religious leaders, formed the background of this study of Jewish life and family patterns in suburbia.

Gordon, Milton M.
Assimilation in American Life. New York: Oxford University Press, 1964

This book is primarily concerned with problems of prejudice and discrimination arising out of differences in race, religion, and national background among the various groups which make up the American people. Jews are included in this analysis (pp. 173-195).

Hapgood, Hutchins
The Spirit of the Ghetto: Studies of the Jewish Quarter of New York. Cambridge: Harvard University Press, 1967

These essays by a non-Jewish author, discussing the Jewish life in New York, appeared in 1902 in American journals. Added notes and commentary by Harry Golden.

Hindus, Milton, ed.
The Old East Side: An Anthology. Philadelphia: Jewish Publication Society of America, 1969

Family life is portrayed in these selections from sixteen authors who describe in various literary forms the "Jewish ghetto" of New York City from 1881 to 1924.

Kramer, Judith R., and **Seymour Leventman**
Children of the Gilded Ghetto. New Haven and London: Yale University Press, 1961

A candid close-up of three generations of American Jews in a midwestern American City – the problems they face, and the conflicts between generations.

Lipman, Eugene J., and **Albert Vorspan**
A Tale of Ten Cities: The Triple Ghetto in American Religious Life. New York: Union of American Hebrew Congregations, 1962

The way in which Protestants, Catholics, and Jews are relating in ten American cities is examined in some detail. The cities chosen for this study represent a cross-section of America. The authors try to answer several important questions dealing with interfaith relations.

Poll, Solomon
The Hasidic Community of Williamsburg. New York: The Free Press, 1962

A sociological study of the ultra-religious Jewish Hasidic community of Williamsburg, New York, which was transplanted from Hungary. The family life of this group is examined in detail.

Ringer, Benjamin
The Edge of Friendliness. New York: Basic Books, 1967

Subtitled "A Study of Jewish-Gentile Relations," this Volume II in the Lakeville Studies explores the relations between Jew and Gentile in Lakeville as they participate in the activities of the community.

Rose, Peter I., ed.
The Ghetto and Beyond: Essays on Jewish Life in America. New York: Random House, 1969

Twenty-six contributors examine the family patterns, political life, and ethnic relationships in the American Jewish community.

Sanders, Ronald
The Downtown Jews: Portrait of an Immigrant Generation. New York: Harper and Row, 1970

A full account of the Yiddish world of New York City during the early part of the twentieth century.

Sanua, Victor D.
"A Study of the Adjustment of Sephardic Jews in the New York Metropolitan Area," *Jewish Journal of Sociology,* IX (June 1967), 25-33

Approximately 40,000 Sephardic Jews reside in the New York City area. The author interviewed 150 of these Syrian families and 36 of the Egyptian families. The adaptive patterns of these families is discussed.

Sanua, Victor D.
"A Review of Social Science Studies on Jews and Jewish Life in the United States," *Journal for the Scientific Study of Religion,* IV (December 1964), 71-83

A brief review of social science studies about Jews in America in the areas of demography, religious and philanthropic values, acculturation and identification, social mobility, political orientation, and psychological adjustment. The review demonstrates that there has been an increase in the publication of such studies in the past ten years, but that studies are still inadequate because of their limited scope.

Sanua, Victor D.
"Patterns of Identification with the Jewish Community in the U.S.A.," *The Jewish Journal of Sociology,* VI (1964), 190-211

A review of studies of attitudes and motivations of Jews which bear on patterns of identification with the Jewish community and participation in Jewish community services and activities.

Schoener, Allan, ed.
Portal to America. New York: Holt, Rinehart and Winston, 1967

A documentary history of Jewish life in the lower East Side of New York during the early 1900s.

Shapiro, Judah S.
"How Democratic Is the Jewish Community?," *Viewpoint,* I (Fall 1965), 8-15

Here Shapiro considers and rejects the theory that there is no Jewish community government in America and that the community is democratic. He describes the organization of the Jewish community in terms of a ruling elite and a non-influential majority, and cautions against the harmful consequences of this type of organization.

Sherman, C. Bezalel
The Jew within American Society: A Study in Ethnic Individuality. Detroit: Wayne University Press, 1965

Serving as a reference work for students in the field of social theory, this book presents data on Jewish demographic, economic, social, and cultural progress in the United States.

Sklare, Marshall, ed.
The Jews: Social Patterns of an American Group. Glencoe, Ill.: The Free Press, 1958

Thirty-three selections discuss the Jewish community, demographic data, religious patterns, psycho-social aspects of life, and cultural patterns. The following selections deal with aspects of Jewish family life: Goldberg and Sharp, 107-118; Strodbeck, 147-168; Rosen, 336-346; Werner and Srole, 347-356; Wolfenstein, 520-534; Robinson, 535-542.

Sklare, Marshall, and **Joseph Greenblum**
Jewish Identity on the Suburban Frontiers. New York: Basic Books, 1967

Subtitled "A Study of Group Survival in the Open Society," this is Vol. I of the Lakeville Studies Series. The community studied is a suburban, middle-class Protestant community with a Jewish minority. This volume of the study analyzes the internal life of the Jewish community – the relationship of the Jews to their heritage, to Israel, to organizations, their fellow Jews, and to their children.

Yaffe, James
The American Jews: Portrait of a Split Personality. New York: Paperback Library, 1969

A detailed picture of Jewish life in America today, dealing with the changing patterns of the Jewish community and family life.

Children and Youth

Bardis, Panos D.
"Religiosity among Jewish Students in a Metropolitan University," *Sociology and Social Research,* XLIX (October 1964), 90-95

In this investigation certain factors that might affect the dependent variable of religiosity were treated as independent variables: familism, dating and liberalism, age, birth order, sex, parental occupation.

Bernstein, Philip, ed.
Youth Looks at the Jewish Community: A Symposium. New York: Council of Jewish Federations and Welfare Funds, 1965

The contributors to this symposium are all young people who write about the meaning of the Jewish way of life to young Jews in an attempt to make the attitudes of young people understandable to their elders.

Bikel, Theodore
"Report on Jewish Campus Youth," *Congress Bi-Weekly,* October 28, 1968, pp. 10-16

Based on formal and informal contacts with Jewish youth over a two-year period, this report is an evaluation of campus experience in terms of Jewish identity.

B'nai B'rith Hillel Foundation
Campus 1966: Change and Challenge. Washington, D.C., 1966

This volume presents the major paper and the reports of a National Conference of Hillel Directors held in December 1965. The topics under discussion include intermarriage and the Jewish college student, the changing campus, and the changing Jewish community.

Boroff, David
"Jewish Teen-Age Culture," *The Annals,* CCCXXXVIII (November 1961), 79-90

The attitudes of Jewish teen-agers toward social, cultural, and religious Jewish values in America are discussed and analyzed.

Brown, Irving R., and **Ralph Segalman**
"Expectant Behavior and Knowledge of Jewish Ethics among Jewish Adolescents," *The Jewish Social Work Forum,* III (Fall 1966), 44-69

This article examines the extent to which Jewish adolescents believe that the Jewish ethics they learned are the basis of their behavior in a number of everyday situations.

Brutman, Seymour, and **David Saltman**
"Sex Education in the Jewish Community Center," *Jewish Social Work Forum,* V (Fall 1968), 58-71

A summary of a sex education program introduced for parents and children (9th-graders) at the Y.M.H.A. in Newark, New Jersey.

Butchik, Allen
"Self-Esteem and Jewish Identification," *Your Child,* II (Winter 1969), 4-13

The research on which this article was based was carried out with a large number of Jewish teen-agers from Orthodox, Conservative, Reform, and unaffiliated backgrounds.

Chaiklin, Harris
"Whose Generation Gap?," *The Jewish Social Work Forum,* VI (Spring 1969), 47-54

One man's answer to the nature of the "generation gap" suggests that the rejection or abandonment of parents by their children is really a two-way process. The author suggests some ways of dealing with the situation.

Coleman, James S.
The Adolescent Society. New York: The Free Press, 1963

In this study of ten high schools, the author observes that Jewish teen-agers over-achieve, relative to Protestants and Catholics, in a number of areas including social as well as scholastic activities.

Dinerman, Miriam
"Some Socio-Cultural Patterns of Jewish Teen-agers," *Jewish Social Service Quarterly,* XXXI (March 1955), 353-358

A study of 210 Jewish middle-class teen-agers in the City of New York who came to the Jewish Neighborhood Center.

Elovitz, Mark H.
"Our Jewish Dropouts," *Your Child,* II (Winter 1969), 21-26

A rabbi discusses what he feels to be the deplorably low level of Jewish education of the huge majority of American Jewish youth. He suggests various reforms which center around the ceremony of Bar Mitzvah and its requirements, and urges the commitment of children to continuing Jewish education.

Ephraim, Miriam
"Meeting the Needs of Today's Jewish Teen-Agers," *Journal of Jewish Communal Service,* XXXVI (Fall 1959), 22-31

A portion of the article discusses the problems of parents in meeting the ever-changing needs of their teen-age children.

Feingold, Norman
"New Challenges in Counseling Jewish College Youth," *Journal of Jewish Communal Service,* XLIII (March 1967), 237-244

Includes a short section on the role of Jewish parents in the behavior modifications of their adolescents.

Feinstein, Sara
"A New Jewish Voice on Campus," *Dimensions,* IV (Winter 1970), 4-23

An examination of the Jewish radical students on the North American campus, with an analysis of the new radical Jewish newspapers.

Feldstein, Donald
"The Jewish College Student and the Jewish Community," *Jewish Community Center Program Aids,* XXXI (Spring 1970), 2-16

A brief description of the contemporary Jewish college student, and the approaches Jewish community centers have made to college youths.

Glazer, Nathan
"The Jewish Role in Student Activism," *Fortune,* January 1969, pp. 111-113, 126-129

The Jewish role in student activism grows from an ancient combination of scholarship and liberalism, compounded by a mistrust of large organizations.

Grad, Eli, ed.
The Teen-ager and Jewish Education. New York: Educators Assembly of the United Synagogue of America, 1968

This is the fourth in a series of annual yearbooks of the Educators Assembly. It brings together articles presenting the various factors which affect the adolescent's relationship to Jewish education.

Greenberg, Irving
"Jewish Survival and the College Campus," *Congress Bi-Weekly,* October 28, 1968, pp. 5-10

Because such a large percentage of Jewish youth attend college, Greenberg maintains, the future of the Jewish community is dependent upon what takes place on American college campuses. He feels, for several specified reasons, that this is not a happy prospect at this time, and suggests ways in which the situation can be improved.

Gross, Morris
Learning Readiness in Two Jewish Groups: A Study in Cultural Deprivation. New York: Center for Urban Education, 1967. For discussion of Ashkenazic and Sephardic Jewish differences, see also, Abraham Shumsky. *The Clash of Cultures in Israel.* New York: Teachers College Press, 1955

A comparative study of the learning readiness of the children of American Sephardic (Syrian descent) and Ashkenazic (European descent) Jewish families in New York City. The sample consisted of 48 Sephardic children and 42 Ashkenazic children.

Israel, Richard J.
"Is This a Job for a Nice Jewish Boy?," *Dimensions in American Judaism,* III (Summer 1969), 33-35

Rabbi Israel expounds a personal theory developed after many years of counseling Jewish students, which postulates that Judaism as a religion is not the only measure for Jewish survival. There are other characteristics which can be used as a measure, and these are often reflected in the types of professions Jews choose.

Jospe, Alfred
"The Sense of Jewish Identity of the Jewish College Student," *Orah Magazine,* November 1965, 19-21

An overview of the marginal loyalties to Jewishness of American Jewish college students.

Lennard, Henry Loeblowitz
"Jewish Youth Appraising Jews and Jewishness," *Yivo Annual of Jewish Social Science,* II-III (1947-1948), 262-281

A questionnaire was administered to 105 Jewish college students relating to their image of a Jew, their Jewish values, and their reaction to anti-Semitism. The results are discussed.

Rosen, Bernard Carl
Adolescence and Religion: The Jewish Teen-ager in American Society. Cambridge, Mass.: Schenkman Publishing, 1965

The religious attitudes and behavior of Jewish adolescents in four American cities were examined in order to understand the social psychology of attitude and behavior formation. In all, 859 adolescents were covered beginning in 1948, with the final sample being taken in 1963.

Rothchild, Sylvia
"Havvrath Shalom: Community without Conformity," *Hadassah Magazine,* June 1970, pp. 11, 24-25

"Havvrath Shalom" (Brotherhood of Peach) is a group of Jewish youth in Boston seeking a fresh religious experience within Judaism and a new Jewish life style relevant to present-day society.

Sanua, Victor D.
"The Jewish Adolescent," *Jewish Education,* XXXVIII (June 1968), 36-52

Several trends emerge from this review of empirical research on Jewish adolescents, starting as early as 1934 but with greater emphasis on more recent work: strengthening or weakening of affiliative tendencies, and differences between gentile and Jewish adolescents, particularly in areas of education and delinquency and other types of deviant behavior.

Sanua, Victor D.
"Jewish Education and Attitudes of Jewish Adolescents," in *Educators Assembly Yearbook, 1967.* Ed. by Eli Grad. New York: United Synagogue of America, 1968, pp. 112-138

The relationship between the extent of Jewish education and the degree of Jewish identification was studied in a large group of Jewish high school students, half of whom had a high level of Jewish education and half, a comparatively low level. Generally, a positive correlation was found between the amount of Jewish education and the strength of identification.

Sebald, Hans
Adolescence: A Sociological Analysis. New York: Appleton-Century-Crofts, 1968

Chapter II contains a review of existing studies related to American Jewish teenagers.

Shapiro, Solomon
"Guidance Needs of the Jewish Teen-ager," *Journal of Jewish Communal Service,* XLV (Summer 1969), 303-308

The article deals briefly with parent-child friction and pressures around the area of the child's educational and career choices.

"Symposium: Jewish Youth and the Sexual Revolution"
Dimensions in American Judaism, III (Winter 1968-1969), 16-28

Articles by Jewish and non-Jewish clergy, marriage counselors, and a sex educator deal with the challenge presented to old standards by the "new" sexual morality. These articles are a direct response to a letter by a young college student seeking a redefinition of morality in all sex relations.

Weisburg, Harold
"Youth Is Asking: Why Be a Jew?," *National Jewish Monthly,* LXXXIII (October 1968), 4-6

According to Dr. Weisburg, the new middle-class Jewish community under the dominantly non-Jewish influence of mass culture is rapidly losing its traditional flavor of Jewishness. Jewish youth, as a result, lack emotional conviction in their sense of Jewish identification.

Zimmer, Uriel
The Jewish Adolescent: A Guide for Today's Girl. New York: Reisel Zimmer, 1963

An Orthodox rabbi discusses the female Jewish adolescent and the religious obligations related to personal behavior.

Family

Appleberg, Esther
"Some Observations on Conflict Change," *The Jewish Social Work Forum,* VI (Fall 1969), 4-22

The dilemma of living as a Jew in America is reviewed. The analysis includes Jewish family life, the college student, the generation gap, and the transmission of values.

Balswick, Jack
"Are American Jewish Families Closely Knit?: A Review of the Literature," *Jewish Social Studies,* XXVIII (July 1966), 159-167

A review of the existing literature of the past twenty years. The author feels that very little empirical research dealing with the question of the American Jewish family has been done.

Bardis, Panos D.
"Familism among Jews in Suburbia," *Social Science,* XXXVI (June 1961), 190-196

Attitudes toward familism of 80 Jewish couples residing in a suburb of a midwestern city were studied to ascertain the degree of association between familism and certain independent variables such as sex, age, number of children, education, and religiosity, and to compare the findings with non-Jewish groups.

Birmingham, Stephen
Our Crowd: The Great Jewish Families of New York. New York: Dell Publishing, 1968

A picture of the growth of the wealthy and well-known Jewish families in New York City during the eighteenth and nineteenth centuries.

Bressler, Marvin
"Selected Family Patterns in W. I. Thomas' Unfinished Study of the 'Bintl Brief'." *American Sociological Review,* XVII (October 1952), 563-571

The "Bintl Brief," meaning a pack of letters, was a "letter to the editor" column, introduced in 1960 in the Yiddish press of New York, in which the correspondents sought information, advice, and comfort in their family and living problems. The author reviews briefly the Jewish family patterns which emerged from these letters.

Foner, Lorraine
"Some Sociological Explanations for the Increased Jewish Membership in Religious Institutions in the Suburbs," *The Jewish Social Work Forum,* III (Fall 1966), 70-83

The desire of parents to provide their children with a Jewish education and identification, the necessity felt by American Jews for survival, identification with the total Jewish community, and social life are some of the motivations examined in the growth of membership in suburban synagogues.

Goldscheider, Calvin, and **Sidney Goldstein**
"Generational Changes in Jewish Family Structure," *Journal of Marriage and the Family,* XXIX (May 1967), 267-276

This paper focuses on family differences of Jews and non-Jews; generational changes in the Jewish family; and differential family structure within the Jewish population. Data were obtained from a random sample of the Providence, Rhode Island, Jewish community.

Goldscheider, Calvin, and **Peter R. Ulenberg**
"Minority Group Status and Fertility," *American Journal of Sociology,* LXXIV (January 1969), 361-372

Most studies of minority group fertility, according to the authors, assume that the differences in fertility will become less distinct as the group acculturates to the majority, and that these differences have little to do with "ethnicity." The authors feel that this theory is not completely accurate. Their study investigates the hypothesis that even under given social and economic changes and concomitant acculturation, the insecurities and marginality associated with minority group status exert an independent effect on fertility.

Hofstein, Saul, Manheim S. Shapiro, and **Louis A. Berman**
"The Jewish Family in a Changing Society: A Symposium," *Dimensions in American Judaism,* IV (Fall 1969), 14-23

Three authors discuss changing family life of Jews in America. Hofstein gives a short summary of how family forms have changed; Shapiro examines the role of the Jewish mother; and Berman relates the shtetl family to American Jewish family life.

Hurvitz, Nathan
"Sources of Motivation and Achievement of American Jews," *Jewish Social Studies,* XXIII (October 1961), 217-234

A paper showing socio-historical, interpersonal, and motivation roots to the upward mobility of American Jews.

Joffe, Natalie F.
The American Jewish Family: A Study. New York: The National Council of Jewish Women, 1954

This booklet presents a composite picture of Jewish family patterns in the United States, covering such areas as marriage, home and family, and community service. Joffe draws her own conclusions on the strength of the Jewish family tie. Included in the study is a guideline for discussion groups.

Kagan, Henry E.
"The Jewish Family," *CCAR Journal,* October 1954, pp. 10-17

Kagan maintains that the American Jewish family, which is predominantly middle class, both acculturates to the American middle-class family and seeks to retain its own distinctive family patterns. He outlines the various characteristics of the middle-class family, points out how the Jewish family is similar, but also clarifies the ways in which it is different. The Jewish families discussed here are of East European heritage.

Landis, Judson T.
"Religiousness, Family Relationships, and Family Values in Protestant, Catholic, and Jewish Families," *Marriage and Family Living,* XXII (November 1960), 341-347

The sample for this study consisted of 2,654 subjects (904 males and 1,750 females) who were university students in family sociology courses. Of these, 9.3 percent were Jewish. The study examined the correlation of family religiousness and family success.

Schwartz, Gwen Gibson, and **Barbara Wyden**
The Jewish Wife. New York: Peter H. Wyden, 1969

A random sample of 200 Jewish wives in Eastern U.S. Metropolitan areas and 200 non-Jewish wives in the same neighborhoods were asked 70 personal questions, followed by intensive interviews with 50 of the Jewish wives. Many of the myths surrounding the Jewish wife are explored and exploded.

Slater, Miriam K.
"My Son the Doctor: Aspects of Mobility among American Jews," *American Sociological Review,* XXXIV (June 1969), 359-373

The rapidity and breadth of Jewish upward mobility in the United States is often ascribed, at least in part, to a value brought over from the East European shtetl, i.e., the importance of learning. Slater believes this explanation to be a myth. She feels that Jews arrive, however poor, with the middle-class orientation towards professionalism, and that this is the factor which influences their success. She provides research to support her hypothesis.

Steinbaum, I.
"A Study of Jewishness of Twenty New York Families," *Yivo Annual of Jewish Social Science,* V (1950), 232-255

A survey of 20 middle-class Jewish families and the factors of "Jewishness" which played an important role in their home life.

Strodtbeck, Fred L.
"Family Interaction, Values and Achievements," in David C. McClelland, *et al.*, eds. *Talent and Society.* New York: Van Nostrand, 1958, pp. 135-194

A comparative study of family interaction and decision-making in a sample of Jewish and Italian families.

Wessel, Bessie Bloom
"Ethnic Family Patterns: The American Jewish Family," *American Journal of Sociology,* LIII (May 1948), 439-442

A short review of existing trends of factors related to American Jewish families at the time of the publication of this paper.

FAMILY LIFE IN CANADA

Belkin, Simon
Through Narrow Gates. Montreal: Eagle Publishing, 1966

A review of Jewish immigration, colonization, and immigrant aid work in Canada from 1840 to 1940.

Chiel, Arthur A.
The Jews of Manitoba. Toronto: University of Toronto Press, 1961

Under the sponsorship of the Manitoba Historical Society, this history is drawn from newspaper accounts, research in archives, and interviews, and highlights the contributions made by the Jewish families who settled in Manitoba to provincial and national life in business, the professions, and the arts.

Kage, Joseph
With Faith and Thanksgiving. Montreal: Eagle Publishing, 1962

This is the story of Jewish immigration and immigrant aid work in Canada, from early settlement through the two World Wars, with the problem of Displaced Persons, to the present day.

Lappin, Ben
The Redeemed Children. Toronto: University of Toronto Press, 1963

A chronicle of 1,116 war orphans who were rescued and resettled in Canada through the collective efforts of a community of 200,000 people. The book highlights the effectiveness of the rescue, which saved a number of those destined to be among Canada's outstanding citizens of today.

Rose, Albert, ed.
A People and Its Faith. Toronto: University of Toronto Press, 1959

Fourteen essays deal with Jews and Reform Judaism in a changing Canada. Some are historical in nature, some deal with contemporary issues, some reveal the essence of Jewish existence, and some deal with the faith of Reform Judaism.

Rosenberg, Louis
"A Preliminary Study of the Number of Jewish Children of Elementary School Age and Jewish Teen-agers in Canada and Its Larger Jewish Communities." *Research Papers.* Series A, No. 5. Montreal: Canadian Jewish Congress, 1966

The statistics in this study are based on the official census statistics of 1961. In addition to these figures, the author has made an estimate of the number of Jewish children of elementary school age in Canada in 1966.

Rosenberg, Louis
"The Number, Age and Sex Distribution and Marital Status of Jews 60 Years of Age and Over in the Metropolitan Census Area of Montreal and in the Larger Municipal Areas within Metropolitan Montreal in 1961." *Research Papers.* Series A, No. 6. Montreal: Canadian Jewish Congress, 1966

The statistics in this paper were gathered to be of special help to social welfare agencies.

Rosenberg, Louis
"Changes in the Geographical Distribution of the Jewish Population of Metropolitan Montreal in the Decennial Periods from 1901 to 1961 and the Estimated Changes during the Period from 1961 to 1971." *Research Papers.* Series A, No. 7. Montreal: Canadian Jewish Congress, 1966

Up to 1961 the Jewish population in Montreal has increased to 102,726. The geographical mobility within the city is described.

Rosenberg, Louis
"A Study of the Changes in the Population Characteristics in the Jewish Community in Canada, 1931-1961," *Canadian Jewish Population Studies,* II (1965). Montreal: Canadian Jewish Congress, 1965

The history of the Canadian Jewish community between 1931 and 1961 is provided, with statistics of age distribution, marital status, intermarriage, mother tongue, and official language spoken, size of family, etc.

Rosenberg, Louis
"The Demography of the Jewish Population in Canada," *Jewish Journal of Sociology,* I (December 1959), 217-233

The study covers the population growth and decrease, immigration, geographical distribution, marital status, marriage rate, intermarriage, size of family, occupational distribution, etc. of the Canadian Jewish community.

Rosenberg, Stuart E.
"Canada's Jews: The Sacred and the Secular," *Conservative Judaism,* XXIV (Spring 1970), 34-44

A short review of the life of 289,000 Jews in Canadian society. American influences on Canadian Jews are also described.

Seeley, John R., R. Alexander, and **E. W. Loosley**
Crestwood Heights. Toronto: University of Toronto Press, 1956

A study of the culture of suburban life in the metropolitan area of Toronto, Canada. The suburb under study contains a 50 percent Jewish population, whose family patterns are analyzed as part of the total investigation.

FAMILY LIFE IN ASIA, AFRICA, LATIN AMERICA

Beller, Jacob
Jews in Latin America. New York: Jonathan David Publishers, 1969

The author, a journalist, explores in detail Jewish life in South America, Central America, Mexico, and the West Indies from the fifteenth century to the present day.

Bensimon-Donat, Doris
"North African Jews in France: Their Attitudes to Israel," *Dispersion and Unity,* No. 10 (Winter 1970), 119-135

A study of 315 adults, 134 working youths, and 180 students from North Africa, who had settled in France. The author examined their feelings about their Jewish identity and their attitudes toward Israel.

Brauer, Erich
"The Jews of Afghanistan," *Jewish Social Studies,* IV (April 1942), 121-138

Report on all aspects of Jewish Afghanistan life, including marriage customs, women, and children.

Hacohen, Devorah, and **Menahem Hacohen**
One People. New York: Funk and Wagnalls, 1969

The story of the Eastern Jews from North Africa, Asia, and Southeastern Europe. Illustrated with many photographs. Family patterns are briefly described.

Magnarella, Paul
"A Note on Aspects of Social Life among the Jewish Kurds of Sanandy, Iran," *The Jewish Journal of Sociology,* XI (June 1969), 51-58

Includes a review of household and family units, housing, and marriage patterns.

Pratt, Emmanuel
"Jewish Communities in China," *Hadassah Magazine,* Parts I, II, III (January, February, March 1970)

Jewish life in China from the Russo-Japanese war to the Communist-Chinese regime. Family life and customs are covered in this series of articles.

Rozin, Mordecai
"The Juridical Home: A Traditional Approach to Marital Counseling," *The Jewish Social Work Forum,* V (Spring 1968), 20-26

This paper describes a practice of dealing with marital difficulties – a practice that persisted in the Iraqi community until 1951, when almost the entire community of Jews from Iraq, consisting of approximately 150,000 people, emigrated to Israel.

Strizower, Schifra
Exotic Jewish Communities. New York: Thomas Yoseloff, 1962

A social anthropologist discusses the life of Jews in Yemen and India, as well as the life of the Karaites and the Sumaritans. Family patterns are included in the author's description of these exotic communities.

THE HOLOCAUST AND FAMILY LIFE

Aichinger, Ilse
Herod's Children. New York: Atheneum, 1963

The story of a group of children who sought, often through fantasies and daydreams, to assuage the pain and horror of Nazi persecution and the allied bombings of World War II.

Bryks, Rachmil
A Cat in the Ghetto. New York: Bloch Publishing, 1959

Four true stories depict the horrors and indignities that fathers, mothers, and boys and girls underwent prior to their death by the Nazis in Auschwitz concentration camp.

Donat, Alexander
The Holocaust Kingdom. New York: Holt, Rinehart and Winston, 1965

The memoirs of a Polish Jewish family which survived the Warsaw ghetto and Hitler's death camps.

Frank, Anne
Diary of a Young Girl. New York: Pocket Books, 1965

A young girl's diary reveals the day-by-day life of a group of Jews living in hiding during the Nazi occupation of Amsterdam.

Friedlander, Albert H., ed.
Out of the Whirlwind: A Reader of Holocaust Literature. New York: Union of American Hebrew Congregations, 1968

Thirty-four selections deal with various aspects of Jewish experience during the Nazi occupation of Europe and the destruction of six million Jews. The selections include parts of personal diaries.

Glatstein, Jacob, Israel Knox, and **Samuel Margoshes,** eds.
Anthology of Holocaust Literature. Philadelphia: Jewish Publication Society of America, 1969

Sixty selections present the varied personal experiences of Jews in the concentration camps and ghettos during World War II under the Nazi occupation and persecution.

Goldstein, Bernard
The Stars Bear Witness. New York: Viking, 1949

A personal narrative of the Jewish populace's attempts to survive the Warsaw ghetto uprising by one of the few who succeeded.

Hart, Kitty
I Am Alive. London: Abelard-Schuman, 1961

A personal narrative of a young woman's experiences in a concentration camp.

Heimler, Eugene
Concentration Camp (original title, *Night of the Mist*). New York: Pyramid Books, 1961

Recalls the captivity of the author, a former Hungarian poet, in the concentration camps of Buchenwald and Auschwitz.

Kaplan, Chaim
Scroll of Agony. Trans. by Abraham I. Katsh. New York: Macmillan, 1965

The diary of a Hebrew educator written during the Nazi occupation of the Warsaw ghetto.

Katzetnik (pseud.)
House of Dolls. Trans. from Hebrew by Moshe M. Kohn. New York: Simon and Schuster, 1955

Based on an authentic diary of a young girl's life in the ghetto, in labor camps, and finally in the "House of Dolls" – a house of prostitution.

Kuper, Jack
Child of the Ghetto. Garden City: Doubleday, 1968

Memories of childhood experiences in occupied Poland during World War II.

Levin, Nora
The Holocaust: The Destruction of European Jewry, 1933-1945. New York: Thomas Y. Crowell, 1968

A comprehensive work on the extermination of the Jews in Europe.

Pawlowicz, Sala
I Will Survive. New York: W. W. Norton, 1962

Stories by and about survivors of the Nazi concentration camps.

Ringelblum, Emmanuel
Notes from the Warsaw Ghetto. New York: McGraw-Hill, 1958

Day-by-day eyewitness accounts by the man who was best equipped to keep that account – the archivist of the Warsaw ghetto.

Vrba, Rudolph, and **Alan Bestic**
I Cannot Forgive. New York: Grove Press, 1964

The story of Dr. Rudolf Vrba's suffering during the two years in Auschwitz, as told to Alan Bestic.

Weinstock, Earl, and **Herbert Wilner**
The Seven Years. New York: Dutton, 1959

Reminiscences of childhood and youth in a concentration camp by a survivor.

FAMILY LIFE IN ISRAEL

Antonovsky, Aaron, and **David Katz**
Americans and Canadians in Israel: A Report. Jerusalem: The Israel Institute of Applied Social Research, 1969. 3 reports

An examination of 2,400 persons who came to Israel prior to March 1966 from Canada and the United States. Part I deals with their home background; Part II with the process of migration; Part III with post-migration mobility patterns; Part IV with adjustment problems; and Part V with integration into Israeli life.

Bachi, Roberta, and **Judah Matras**
"Family Size Preferences of Maternity Cases in Israel," *The Milbank Memorial Fund Quarterly,* XLII (April 1964), 38-56

How many children do Israeli women want and what are the factors influencing their desires? are questions this study attempts to answer. Some of the variables studied are age, education, country of birth, employment experience, religious tie, and the practice of contraception.

Blake, Howard
"A City Kibbutz," *Israel Magazine,* II (1970), 59-67

A description of a new experimental way of life – the city kibbutz – for a group of North Americans, including family life patterns.

Eaton, Joseph W.
"Reaching the Hard-to-Reach in Israel," *Social Work,* XV (January 1970), 85-96

An analysis of voluntary programs for children of Afro-Asian families, the poor, and the culturally-deprived, in a section of Tel Aviv.

Eisenstadt, S. N.
"The Oriental Jews in Israel," *Jewish Social Studies,* XII (July 1950), 199-222

Study of some of the social problems and processes of the Oriental Jewish family in Israel.

Foa, Uriel G.
"A Standardized Multiple-Factor of Socio-Economic Status for Jerusalem Jewish Families," *Jewish Social Studies,* X (January 1948), 73-76

Development of a scale for measurement of the socio-economic status of Jerusalem Jewish families of the lower and middle classes.

Gabriel, R.
"Some New Data on Age at Marriage in Israel," in *Scripta Hierosolymitana,* III (1956), 248-264

A detailed picture of the differences in age at marriage of various sections of the population of Israel in 1948.

Isaacs, Harold R.
American Jews in Israel. New York: John Day, 1966

Based on interviews with 50 subjects in 1963, this report of the experiences of American Jews who migrated to Israel explores the difficulties faced in their attempt to bridge and combine their American and Jewish identities in Israel.

Jaffe, David Eliezer
"Substitutes for Family: On the Development of Institutional Care for Dependent Children in Israel," *Journal of Jewish Communal Service,* XLIV (Winter 1967), 129-144

A description of the child care services and children's institutions in Israel from 1800 to 1965.

Kleinberger, Ahavin F.
Society, Schools and Progress in Israel. New York: Permagon Press, 1967

A background book related to the present society of Israel including social stratification and education.

Matras, Judah
Social Change in Israel. Chicago: Aldine Publishing, 1965

Chapter V deals with changes in family formation in Israel, and includes census data related to family life.

Matras, Judah
"Religious Observance and Family Formation in Israel: Some Intergenerational Changes," *The American Journal of Sociology,* LXIX (March 1964), 464-475

The relationship between intergenerational change in religious observance and family patterns of women in Israel is investigated in this study.

Pincus, Chasya
Come from the Four Winds: The Story of Youth Aliyah. New York: Herzl Press, 1970

Since its inception in 1934 under the guidance of Recha Freier and the late Henrietta Szold, Youth Aliyah has brought 120,000 young people to Israel, where they helped rebuild the Jewish nation and, in doing so, gave new purpose to their own lives.

Reifen, David
"Some Causative Aspects of Juvenile Delinquency in Israel," *Etgar,* I (Summer 1966), 10-14

A Juvenile Court judge discusses some of the problems of adjustment to Israel of immigrants and their families which lead to juvenile delinquency. It seems that the immigrants from Oriental countries have more problems adjusting to life in Israel, a life based on the societal pattern of the Western world, than those of European or Anglo-Saxon countries, and are thus more highly represented in the courts.

Rosenak, Michael
Israel: Land of Promise. New York: Union of Orthodox Jewish Congregations of America, 1968

An educational resource and guide for Jewish Orthodox youths which covers life in Israel.

Roth, Eleanor
"The Homeland Is Here, Mr. Twain," *Reconstructionist,* XXXV (April 11, 1969), 14-20

A discussion of some of the social problems faced by newly-arrived immigrant families in Israel.

Sachar, Howard Morley
From the Ends of the Earth: The People of Israel. Cleveland and New York: World Publishing, 1964

In a descriptive manner the author tells of the diverse peoples, from Yemen, Egypt, North Africa, Iraq, Europe, and other lands, who have settled in Israel. Their contributions to the country are described through sketches and personal accounts, providing insights into modern Jewish history.

Sachar, Howard Morley
Aliyah: The Peoples of Israel. Cleveland and New York: World Publishing, 1961

Through the device of "biographies" this book deals with the types of people who settled in Palestine before 1948 and helped create the State of Israel. The author describes the various peoples of Israel through the lives of 15 personalities.

Samuel, Edwin
The Structure of Society in Israel. New York: Random House, 1969

An analysis by a British Viscount of the structure of Israel's society including the kibbutz, the ultra-Orthodox groups, urban society, and the Israeli Arabs.

Sherman, Arnold
Impaled on a Cactus Bush: An American Family in Israel. New York: Sabra Books, 1970

An American Jewish family who moved to Israel seven years ago describes their social and personal adjustments to Israel's society.

Spiro, Melford E.
"The Sabras and Zionism: A Study in Personality and Ideology," *Social Problems,* V (Fall 1957), 100-110

The attitudes of a particular group of Sabras toward Jewish culture, history, and nationhood, and towards themselves as Jews is discussed in this article. Some of the ways in which the Sabras' ideology expresses important elements in their personality organization are suggested.

Talmon, Yonina
"Family versus Community: Patterns of Divided Loyalties in Israel," in H. Kent Geiger, ed. *Comparative Perspectives on Marriage and the Family.* Boston: Little, Brown, 1968, pp. 47-67. Also in *International Social Science Journal,* XIV (July 1962), 468-487

An analysis of the impact of radical and rapid social change on patterns of family organization and on the relationship between family and community. The analysis includes the kibbutz (collective settlement), the Moshav (cooperative settlement), and the family in urban centers of Israel.

Talmon, Yonina
"The Family in Israel," *Marriage and Family Living,* XVI (November 1954), 343-349

The inhabitants of Israel are predominantly immigrants from all over the world, who thus present a great variety of patterns of family organization. This paper describes and analyzes the main characteristics of family life in Israel.

Wallfish, Asher
"An Experimental Urban Kibbutz," *Hadassah Magazine,* October 1969, pp. 12-15

A description of a novel way of cooperative living of a group of families and individuals from North America who settled in the town of Carmiel, near Haifa in Israel.

Wolman, B.
"The Social Development of Israeli Youth," *Jewish Social Studies,* XI (July and October 1949), 283-306; 343-372

Study of Israeli youth's friendship and reference groups and moral development from pre-puberty to post-pubescence.

THE KIBBUTZ OF ISRAEL

As a Social Movement

Arian, Alan
Ideological Change in Israel. Cleveland: The Press of Case Western Reserve University, 1968

One of the primary concerns of this study is the change in the kibbutz movement. The emphasis is on the political change related to the place of the kibbutzim in the national political system.

Baratz, Joseph
A Village by the Jordan: The Story of Degania. London: The Harvill Press, 1954

A personal account of the founding of the first kibbutz in Israel, written by one of the "fathers" of this settlement who came from the Ukraine to pioneer in Israel.

Behavior Research in Collective Settlements in Israel
American Journal of Orthopsychiatry, XXVIII (July 1958), 547-598

Six authors discuss the varied aspects of research in the kibbutz of Israel.

Ben-Yosef, Avraham
The Purest Democracy in the World. New York: Thomas Yoseloff, 1963

A description of the day-to-day life in a modern Israeli kibbutz by a British immigrant to Israel who settled on a kibbutz. Three chapters are devoted to the individual, the family, and women in the kibbutz. The Appendix contains a list of kibbutzim in Israel in 1961.

Bentwich, Norman
"The Collective Settlements of Israel," in N. Bentwick, ed. *A New Way of Life.* London: Shindler and Golomb, 1949, pp. 8-27

The collective settlements in Israel can trace succession from a small branch of the Jewish people, the sect of the Essenes, who dwelt in collective communities. In the latter part of the nineteenth century, the early Zionists looked to Palestine as a place where a just social order could be created. However, the earliest agricultural settlements of the Jews in Palestine were ordered otherwise. They were villages of individual farmers who employed Arab labor for the rough work in the fields, and who aspired to acquire as their private property the land which had been leased to them by the Zionists.

Cohen, Erik
Bibliography of the Kibbutz. Jerusalem: Hebrew University, Department of Sociology, 1964. Also available from Israel Horizons, Suite 700, 150 Fifth Ave., New York, N.Y., 10011.

A selected bibliography of material in English on the kibbutzim for the period 1954-1964. The list contains about 250 items.

Diamond, Stanley
"Kibbutz and Shtetl: The History of an Idea," *Social Problems,* V (Fall 1957), 68-79

The specific principles and ideological relationships which constitute the kibbutz can be properly understood only with reference to the Eastern European Jewish background of the Vatikim, the veteran settlers. It is against the backdrop of the Vatikim that Dr. Diamond discusses the shtetl, the dominant pattern in Eastern European Jewish culture. The Vatikim were dedicated to the rejection of these Eastern European Jewish cultural patterns.

Drapkin, Darin H.
The Other Society. London: Victor Gollancz, 1962

A complete examination of the kibbutz, including some of the historical developments, structures, social and family life, and the economy.

Efroymson, C. W.
"Collective Agriculture in Israel," *The Journal of Political Economy,* LVIII (February 1950), 30-44

A description of land use by the collective settlements in Israel. A short description of the type of life in the settlement is included.

Eisenstadt, S. N.
Israeli Society. New York: Basic Books, 1967

A sociological analysis of Israeli society and institutions, dealing with such problems as the role of political parties, integration of new immigrants, and struggles between the generations. In dealing with the social structure in Israel the author examines the areas of education, youth, family life, and cultural institutions.

Friedmann, Georges
The End of the Jewish People. New York: Doubleday Anchor Books, 1968

This book, the result of two visits to Israel in 1963 and 1964 by the French author, is a reflection on the past, present, and future of the Jews. It examines the present problems confronting Israel, and depicts an anxious view of the prospects of the Jewish people, with special emphasis on kibbutz life.

Gelb, Saadia
"The Kibbutz Today," *Reconstructionist,* XXX (April 1964), 7-12

The author aims at correcting what she believes are several prevailing misconceptions about kibbutz life. She contends that the kibbutz is a strong and vital institution and its future is bright.

Golan, Shmuel
"Collective Education in the Kibbutz," *Psychiatry,* XXII (May 1959), 167-177

Describes the kibbutz movement as a unique social experiment which began forty or fifty years ago in Palestine and has since grown tremendously. In a kibbutz all property is shared; all work to be done is decided upon by a rotating Labor Arrangement Committee. The social problems of production and distribution are thus met in a manner essentially different from that in capitalistic societies, and, correspondingly, many social and cultural forms have been created which differ from the customary ones.

Israel Magazine
"Life on the Kibbutz." Special issue, I:11 (1969)

Eight articles and a number of photographs review the kibbutz of Israel today. Life on the kibbutzim is described in detail, and present changes are documented.

Kanovsky, Elijahu
The Economy of the Israeli Kibbutz. Cambridge: Harvard University Press, 1968

An analysis of the economy of Israeli kibbutzim in the post-independence period.

Kerem, Moshe
The Kibbutz. Jerusalem: Israel Digest, No. 27, October 1963

A brief history of the kibbutz movement is given in this booklet – its founders and activities, and description of aspects of the kibbutz which are unique to it, such as what a kibbutz is and how it works; who owns and governs it; work hours and activities; child care and family life; cultural life and entertainment; and the ties between the kibbutz and the larger Israel community.

Kishner, Simon
The Village Builder. New York: Herzl Press, 1967

A biography of Abraham Harzfeld, one of the pioneers in establishing agricultural settlements in Israel.

Leon, Dan
The Kibbutz: A Way of Life. New York: Permagon Press, 1969

The author is a member of one of the settlements in Artzi Hashomer Hazair, the largest of the four national federations of kibbutzim in Israel (73 settlements in 1967). Family life in this type of kibbutz is described.

Living in a Kibbutz
Jerusalem: Jewish Agency, 1969

An illustrated booklet which gives a general picture of life in a kibbutz.

Nissenson, Hugh
Notes from the Frontier. New York: Dial Press, 1968

An American who lives in a border kibbutz describes life in the collective settlement during the tense days prior to and during the six-day war in Israel, June 1967

Ophir, Aryeh, Moshe Chizik, and **Dov Maisel,** eds.
The Kibbutz. Tel-Aviv: Misaviv Laolam Publishing House, 1964

Primarily this is a photographic essay dealing with life in the kibbutz; the text gives the reader an overview of the varied aspects of collective living.

Rettig, Solomon, and **Benjamin Pasamanick**
"Some Observations on the Moral Ideology of First and Second Generation Collective and Non-Collective Settlers in Israel," *Social Problems,* XI (Fall 1963), 165-178

This study attempts to delineate some aspects of the collective settlers' moral ideology, and to contrast these with the ideology of non-collective settlers. It also tests the hypothesis that the collective settlers were successful in transmitting and preserving the different aspects of their ideology to the second generation.

Rosenfeld, Eva
"The American Social Scientist in Israel: A Case Study in Role Conflict," *American Journal of Orthopsychiatry,* XXVIII (July 1958), 563-571

The author describes some of her experiences while doing research in various kibbutzim. These experiences have to do with her role as "observer" and the unique problems faced.

Rosenfeld, Eva
"Institutional Changes in the Kibbutz," *Social Problems,* V (1957), 110-136

Focuses attention on teen-agers. Two main sources of pressures are described: (1) increased division of labor and role differentiation and decreased prestige of the kibbutz members of the society; and (2) ineffective socialization of the members of the kibbutz, in part due to a strong feeling against the formalization of institutional relations.

Schlesinger, Benjamin
"Israel's Kibbutzim Fashion a New Life." *The Jewish Standard.* December 1, 1969, 16-19, 33-37

A personal account of a summer's visit to Israel and observations on living on a kibbutz.

Schwartz, Richard D.
"Some Problems of Research in Israeli Settlements," *American Journal of Orthopsychiatry,* XXVIII (July 1958), 572-576

The author outlines various methods of research which are appropriate to field work in Israeli settlements, and which by their design help to reduce the area within which bias can operate.

Schwartz, Richard D.
"Democracy and Collectivism in the Kibbutz," *Social Problems,* V (1957), 137-147

Calls attention to an assessment of the political and economic systems of the kibbutz. The evidence tends to support the belief that democracy can exist in a collective society without ownership of private property.

Spiro, Melford E.
Kibbutz: Venture in Utopia. Cambridge: Harvard University Press, 1956

One of the earliest studies of the kibbutz by an American anthropologist. It is a case study of one kibbutz completed in 1951, with an examination of the family patterns in that setting.

Stern, Boris
The Kibbutz That Was. Washington, D.C.: Public Affairs Press, 1965

The theme of this volume is the changes that have taken place in the organization and activities of the kibbutz in the late 1950s and early 1960s.

Talmon, Yonina
"Differentiation in Collective Settlements," in *Scripta Hierosolymitana.* vol. III. Ed. by Roberto Bachi. Jerusalem: Magnes Press, Hebrew University, 1956, 153-178

A description and analysis of an explorative research project dealing with elite formation in collective settlements.

Tamir, Shlomo
Everyday Life in the Kibbutz. Jerusalem: Ahva Press, 1968. Distributed by Jewish Agency

This descriptive booklet deals with work, family life, cultural life, and the general ideological foundations of the kibbutz, written by a man who lived in one for 47 years.

Tauber, Esther
Moulding Society to Man. New York: Bloch Publishing, 1955

An Israeli describes the history of the kibbutz, its development, and the place of the individual in the collective society.

Viteles, Harry
A History of the Cooperative Movement in Israel. London: Valentine Mitchell, 1967. 7 vols.

A detailed analysis of the kibbutz, from its inception in 1909 to the present day. Volume II details the family patterns introduced into the kibbutz.

Viteles, Harry
"Cooperative Agricultural Settlements in Israel," *Sociology and Social Research,* XXXIX (January-February 1955), 171-176

Of the 57,600 farms in Israel at the end of 1952, 38 percent were cooperative agricultural settlements, or *moshavim.* These are to be differentiated from the kibbutzim, the communitarian settlements, with all property vested in the kibbutzim and with all activities, including services such as housing, education, etc., being cooperative. The moshavim and the kibbutzim occupy land that they received from the Jewish National Funds.

Weingarten, Murray
"The Individual and the Community," in Eric and Mary Josephson, eds. *Man Alone.* New York: Dell Publishing, 1962, pp. 516-533

A personal observation of life in a kibbutz by a member of kibbutz Gesher Haziv, including an analysis of the individual in this setting.

Weingarten, Murray
Life in a Kibbutz. Jerusalem: Youth and Hechalutz Department, Zionist Organization, 1959

A former American, now a member of kibbutz Gesher Haziv, describes the problems and satisfactions of living in a kibbutz.

Weintraub, D., M. Lissak, and **Y. Azmon**
Moshava, Kibbutz, and Moshav: Patterns of Jewish Rural Settlement and Development in Palestine. Ithaca: Cornell University Press, 1969

A comparative analysis of the three major types of agricultural settlements developed in Israel: the moshava, based on individual family-owned property; the kibbutz, a communal system; and the moshav, a cooperative type. The kibbutz analysis (pp. 68-122) describes kibbutz Ein Harod founded in 1921.

Family Life in the Kibbutz

Horigan, Francis D.
The Israeli Kibbutz: Psychiatric, Psychological, and Social Studies with Emphasis on Family Life and Structure. Psychiatric Abstract Series #9, May 1962. Bethesda, Maryland: Public Health Service, National Institute of Health

A bibliography of 100 items from book and journal literature, half of which are annotated.

Lucas, Esther
"Family Life in the Kibbutz," in N. Bentwick, ed. *A New Way of Life.* London: Shindler and Golomb, 1949, pp. 54-66

Points out that equality of opportunity for man and woman in all spheres of endeavor in Palestinian collective settlements has in no way militated against the conventional family life. The social set-up which frees the woman from the slavery of household chores has, at the same time, accepted her as wife and mother according to the traditional Jewish beliefs.

Queen, Stuart A., and **Robert W. Habenstein**
"The Minimum Family of the Kibbutz," in Queen and Habenstein, eds. *The Family in Various Cultures.* New York: J. B. Lippincott, 1965, pp. 116-137

A summary of findings related to the family in the kibbutz.

Rosner, Menahem
"Women in the Kibbutz: Changing Status and Concepts," *Asian and African Studies* (An Annual of the Israel Oriental Society), III (1967), 35-68

An analysis of the changes that have occurred with respect to the equality accorded to women in the kibbutz, based on a 1965-66 research project.

Schlesinger, Benjamin
"Family Life in the Kibbutz of Israel: Utopia Gained or Paradise Lost," *International Journal of Comparative Sociology,* XI (December 1970), 1-21

A review of the available literature in English dealing with the family in the kibbutz.

Schlesinger, Benjamin
"Changing Family Life in the Kibbutz of Israel," *Etgar,* I (Winter 1965-66), 21-31

Family life in the kibbutz is described with emphasis on values and ideals different from the conventional family unit. Also included is a brief review of literature on the various aspects of child development discussed.

Shepher, Joseph
"Familism and Social Structure: The Case of the Kibbutz," *Journal of Marriage and the Family,* XXXI (August 1969), 567-573

A comparative study of the different values, division of labor, and social activities in two types of kibbutzim – those with a "collective" housing system, where children live apart from parents, and those with a "familistic" housing system, where children live with their parents. Between 1951 and 1963 nine kibbutzim changed from the collective type to the "familistic" system.

Spiro, Melford E.
"Is the Family Universal?: The Israel Case," in Norman W. Bell, and Ezra F. Vogel, eds. *A Modern Introduction to the Family.* rev. ed. New York: The Free Press, 1968, pp. 68-79. Also in *American Anthropologist,* LVI (October 1954), 839-846

A discussion of Murdock's proposition of the universality of the nuclear family in relation to the family in the kibbutz.

Spiro, Melford E.
"Marriage in the Kibbutz," *American Anthropologist,* LVI (October 1954), 840-842

A description of marriage in the kibbutz and the social-psychological factors related to it.

Talmon, Yonina
"The Family in a Revolutionary Movement: The Case of the Kibbutz in Israel," in M. F. Nimkoff, ed. *Comparative Family Systems.* Boston: Houghton Mifflin, 1965, pp. 259-286

The purpose of this case study of family patterns in a sample of 12 kibbutzim is to discover the interrelation between changes in communal structure and modification of family organization in a collective movement.

Talmon, Yonina
"Mate Selection in Collective Settlements," *American Sociological Review,* XXIX (August 1964), 491-508

An analysis of second-generation exogamy in the kibbutzim in Israel. Examination of this case study provides a crucial test of theories of mate selection.

Talmon, Yonina
"Aging in Israel, a Planned Society," *The American Journal of Sociology,* LXVII (November 1961), 284-295

Aging is a difficult process in the kibbutz, as well as in other settings, because of the emphasis placed in kibbutz ideology on the ability to work. The author describes the process of reorientation and some of the programs that have been set up for the aged in some kibbutzim.

Children and Child Rearing

Bar-Joseph, Rivkah
"Assisting Kibbutz Parents in the Tasks of Child Rearing," in H. Kent Geiger, ed. *Comparative Perspectives on Marriage and the Family.* Boston: Little, Brown, 1968, pp. 159-176. Also in *Human Relations,* XII (1959), 345-360

This paper compares the framework of socialization of the young child in the communal settlements in Israel with the social pattern that frames the life of the adults.

Barnett, Larry D.
"The Kibbutz as a Child Rearing System: A Review of the Literature," *Journal of Marriage and the Family,* XXVII (August 1965), 348-349

This paper summarizes the existing literature concerned with the effects on the behavior of individuals being reared in conjugal families and in Israeli kibbutzim. Research evidence indicates that there are in general no marked differences in deviant behavior rates between the two groups of individuals.

Bettelheim, Bruno
The Children of the Dream. London: Macmillan, 1969

An analysis of the children reared in a kibbutz in Israel at various stages, from birth through adolescence. The sample was obtained mainly from one kibbutz during a seven-week period, with interviews in English with children, parents, and teachers.

Bettelheim, Bruno
"Does Communal Education Work?: The Case of the Kibbutz," *Commentary,* XXXIII (February 1962), 117-126

This article represents Bettelheim's assessment of the processes of communal education in the kibbutz from the literature.

Faigin, Helen
"Social Behavior of Young Children in the Kibbutz," *Journal of Abnormal and Social Psychology,* LVI (1958), 117-129

An exploratory study of the social development of children of toddler age growing up in kibbutzim. Since these children live together in groups practically from birth, the setting is propitious for studying the extent and limits of social interaction among very young people. A secondary point of emphasis is the role of the *metapelet* (children's caretaker) and her relationship with the children.

Gewirtz, Hava B., and **J. L. Gewirtz.**
"Caretaking Settings, Background Events, and Behavior Differences in Four Israeli Child-Rearing Environments: Some Preliminary Trends," in B. M. Foss, ed. *Determinants of Infant Behavior.* vol. IV. London: Methuen, 1967

A functional analysis of the nature of stimuli affecting infants in four child-rearing settings. Babies in conventional families, in kibbutzim, in residential institutions, and in day-care nurseries were observed. Special attention was devoted to the case of each infant as an individual within his own setting.

Gewirtz, J. L.
"The Course of Smiling by Groups of Israeli Infants in the First Eighteen Months of Life," *Scripta Hierosolymitana,* XIV (1965), 9-58

An attempt to chart the age course of the smile response in the first 18 months of life. Certain small differences were found in the infants studied from four different settings in Israel.

Golan, Shmuel
"Collective Education in the Kibbutz," *American Journal of Orthopsychiatry,* XXVIII (July 1958), 549-556

In the kibbutz, all the children live and learn together in peer groups until they are 18 years of age, when they become full-fledged members of the kibbutz. This article describes their collective education.

Gruneberg, Richard
"Education in the Kibbutz," in N. Bentwick, ed. *A New Way of Live.* London: Shindler and Golomb, 1949, pp. 81-89

Kibbutz education has two objectives. First, it strives to make the young a part of the communal life, inculcating the communal way into the child's philosophy from his earliest days. Besides this formation of habits and emotional ties, the second objective is to provide the child with the intellectual tools to form his own opinions.

Halpern, Howard
"Alienation from Parenthood in the Kibbutz and America," *Marriage and Family Living,* XXIV (February 1962), 42-45

A comparison of child rearing in the kibbutz and in America.

Irvine, Elizabeth E.
"Observations on the Aims and Methods of Child Rearing in Communal Settlements in Israel," *Human Relations,* V (1952), 247-275

Calls attention to the emphasis placed on the family as the only satisfactory environment for an infant, and the basic importance of an undisturbed mother-child relationship during the first few years of life. In Israeli communal settlements children are brought up from birth not in the family, but in groups, and not by the parents, but by professionals.

Kaffman, Mordecai
"A Comparison of Psychopathology: Israeli Children from Kibbutz and from Urban Surroundings," *American Journal of Orthopsychiatry,* XXXV (April 1965), 509-520

The author has investigated the comparative psychiatric diagnostic distribution, characteristics, and intensity of emotional pathology in two groups of seriously disturbed kibbutz and urban children, referred for diagnosis and treatment at outpatient clinics.

Mohr, George J.
"A Discussion on Behavior Research in Collectives in Israel," *American Journal of Orthopsychiatry,* XXVIII (July 1958), 584-586

Comments on the observation that in social and inter-personal responsiveness, the child reared in the kibbutz is somewhat retarded as compared with the non-kibbutz reared infant. This retardation, however, is not observed in children 9 to 11 years of age.

Nagler, Shmuel
"Clinical Observations on Kibbutz Children," *The Israel Annals of Psychiatry and Related Disciplines,* I (October 1963), 201-216

No striking differences emerge between the psychopathology of children of kibbutz families and the traditional family in Israel. The mental health facilities for the kibbutz society and the types of disorders found in kibbutz children are described.

Neubauer, Peter B., ed.
Children in Collectives: Child-Rearing Aims and Practices in the Kibbutz. Springfield, Ill.: Charles C. Thomas, 1965

A report of an institute held in Israel during the summer of 1963. The varied topics under discussion included kibbutz education, early childhood, latency, adolescence, family life, and the role of women in the kibbutz system.

Rabin, A. I.
Growing Up in the Kibbutz. New York: Springer Publishing, 1965

A comparison of the personalities of children brought up in the kibbutz and those reared in families. The author's purpose is to present a systematic exploration and interpretation of kibbutz children at several age levels from infancy to maturity.

Rabin, A. I.
"Kibbutz Adolescents," *American Journal of Orthopsychiatry,* XXXI (July 1961), 493-504

Several projective methods were used in this comparative study of kibbutz and non-kibbutz 17-year-olds.

Rabin, A. I.
"Attitudes of Kibbutz Children to Family and Parents," *American Journal of Orthopsychiatry,* XXIX (January 1959), 172-179

Discusses the effects of early childhood experiences upon later personality development and inter-personal relations. Dr. Rabin presents the results of a study of the attitudes of 92 kibbutz-reared fourth- and fifth-grade children from six different villages.

Rabin, A. I.
"Infants and Children under Conditions of 'Intermittent' Mothering in the Kibbutz," *American Journal of Orthopsychiatry,* XXVIII (July 1958), 577-584

The infant in the kibbutz does not experience "continuous" mothering as we know it. This study explores the question of how young infants who experienced "intermittent" mothering in the kibbutz are affected as compared with infants in the conventional nuclear family.

Rabin, A. I.
"Kibbutz Children: Research Findings to Date," *Children,* V (September-October 1958), 179-184

The author discusses the methods of rearing kibbutz children and the research related to various age groups.

Rabin, A. I.
"Some Psychosexual Differences between Kibbutz and Non-Kibbutz Israeli Boys," *Journal of Projective Techniques,* XXII (1958), 328-332

A group of 27 ten-year-old boys was compared with a group of boys raised in patriarchal-type families to investigate the hypothesis that kibbutz boys will experience less intense Oedipal feelings, more diffused positive identification with their fathers, and less sibling rivalry. The hypothesis was supported.

Rabin, A. I.
"The Israeli Kibbutz as a Laboratory for Testing Psychodynamic Hypotheses," *Psychological Record,* VII (1957), 111-115

Particular attention here is focused on child-rearing practices characterized by "partial and intermittent mothering," and hypotheses regarding personality development.

Rabin, A. I.
"Personality Maturity of Kibbutz and Non-Kibbutz Children as Reflected in Rorschach Findings," *Journal of Projective Techniques,* XXI (1957), 48-53

Using the Rorschach method to ascertain certain aspects of personality development, Rabin tests the hypothesis that children reflect several deleterious effects if they experience "maternal deprivation" in infancy and early childhood.

Rapaport, David
"The Study of Kibbutz Education and Its Bearing on the Theory of Development," *American Journal of Orthopsychiatry,* XXVIII (July 1958), 587-597

The various traditional, cultural, historical, economic, and institutional forces which shaped the kibbutz and affected the system of collective education are described and evaluated. The author suggests ways in which this educational system, so different from ours, is adaptable to the peculiar needs of the kibbutz society.

Spiro, Melford E.
Children of the Kibbutz. New York: Schocken Books, 1965

In this revision of the original 1958 edition, the author's aim is to present a structural description of kibbutz socialization and personality patterns.

Spiro, Melford E.
"Education in a Communal Village in Israel," *American Journal of Orthopsychiatry,* XXV (April 1955), 283-292

Discusses the system of education, known as *chinuch meshutaf* or "collective education," as practiced in Kiryat Yedidim, the kibbutz in which this paper was written and in which its research was carried out. The founders of Kiryat Yedidim were Eastern European Jews who had rebelled against the differential status of the sexes, among other things, and against the traditional family structure of both Jewish and European cultures.

Winograd, Marilyn
"The Development of the Young Child in a Collective Settlement," *American Journal of Orthopsychiatry,* XXVIII (July 1958), 557-562

Observations for this paper were collected over a long period of time to describe and evaluate some aspects of the growth and development of a group of young children raised in a kibbutz.

Wolins, Martin
"Group Care: Friend or Foe?," *Social Work,* XIV (January 1969), 35-52

Assumptions about intelligence, personality, and value development of group-reared children are tested in this study, which was conducted in Israel, Austria, Poland, and Yugoslavia. Five different types of group care for children were investigated. The findings show no significant intellectual or psycho-social deficiencies in group-reared children as compared with those raised at home. The author feels that the group setting has potential for changing values.

Wolins, Martin
"Another View of Group Care," *Child Welfare,* XLIV (January 1965), 10-18

A number of countries choose group care as the preferred foster-care method to provide adequate emotional support and appropriate socialization. Wolins describes the Russian and Israeli experience in this area, and suggests several ways in which group care can be implemented in the United States.

Wolins, Martin
"Political Orientation, Social Reality, and Child Welfare," *Social Service Review,* XXXVIII (December 1964), 429-442

This study presents a survey of several types of group care for children in different countries. The author discusses the origins of group care – ideological and circumstantial. He concludes that on the whole, group care in most settings studied is appropriate and beneficial. The kibbutz system is among the settings under comparison.

Wolins, Martin
"Some Theory and Practice in Child Care: A Cross-Cultural View," *Child Welfare,* XLII (October 1963), 368-399

Wolins feels that the American ideal of family care for all children, which stems from the belief that any type of institutional care is inferior if not harmful, needs some rethinking. In this article he discusses the ideological and societal frameworks for group child care in four foreign countries including Israel, and attempts to show their validity and worth.

GENERAL BIBLIOGRAPHIES AND REFERENCES

Leo Baeck Institute
Year Books. New York.

The Institute was founded in 1955 to collect material and sponsor research on the history of the Jewish community in Germany and in other German-speaking countries from the Emancipation to its decline and new dispersion. Each Year Book contains an extensive bibliography of an average of 40 pages which deals with varied aspects of German-Jewish life, including memoirs, community life, etc.

Cedarbaum, Sophia N.
The Bible: A Short Bibliography. New York: Jewish Book Council of America, 1962

One hundred annotated items related to commentaries, history, geography, and basic biblical books.

Council of Jewish Federations and Welfare Funds
A Selected Bibliography of Major Council Publications. New York, 1970

Among the topics covered in this bibliography are items related to Judaism and Jewish identification, Jewish education, college youths, and health and welfare services.

Disenhouse, Phylis
Doctoral Dissertations and Masters' Theses Accepted by American Institutions of Higher Learning, 1964-1965. New York: Yivo Institute for Jewish Research, 1968

A list of 97 annotated doctoral and masters' theses which cover Jewish content in the humanities and the social sciences.

Federbush, Simon, ed.
World Jewry Today. New York: Thomas Yoseloff, 1959

This reference volume covers all Jewish communities and their institutions and populations.

Fine, Morris, and **Milton Himmelfarb,** eds.
American Jewish Yearbook. Philadelphia: Jewish Publication Society of America.

An annual record of events and trends in American and world Jewish Life. Each volume has major essays dealing with special topics of concern to the Jewish community. Demographic data about the Jewish world population is included in each volume.

Graeber, Isacque
"Jewish Themes in American Doctoral Dissertations, 1933-1962," *Yivo Annual of Jewish Social Science,* XIII (1965), 279-304

A total of 452 dissertations on Jewish subjects are listed under topical headings of sociology, psychology, anthropology, and economics. About 15 titles relate to Jewish family life.

Jewish Book Council of America
Selected Bibliography on the Holocaust. New York, 1969

Eighty annotated items related to Jewish experiences during the Nazi Holocaust.

Ravid, Wita
Doctoral Dissertations and Masters' Theses Accepted by American Institutions of Higher Learning, 1963-1964. New York: Yivo Institute for Jewish Research, 1966

An annotated list of 77 doctoral and masters' theses related to Jewish humanities and sociological themes.

Rosten, Leo
The Joys of Yiddish. New York: McGraw-Hill Pocket Books, 1970

This lexicon of Yiddish-in-English contains also definitions related to the family (*mishpocheh*).

Schmelz, V. O., and **P. Glikson,** eds.
Jewish Population Studies, 1961-1968. Jerusalem: Hebrew University, Institute of Contemporary Jewry, 1970

A collection of papers which discuss Jewish population trends, mortality, fertility, and education.

Shunami, Shlomo
Bibliography of Jewish Bibliographies. Jerusalem: Hebrew University Press, 1936 and 1947

A major compilation of Jewish bibliographies.

Silberstein, Vivian
Jewish Life in Many Lands: A Selected Bibliography. New York: Jewish Book Council of America, 1969

Approximately 100 annotated items related to Jewish life in Africa, Asia, Israel, Australia, Europe, Latin America, New Zealand, Canada, and the United States.

Singer, Isidor, ed.
The Jewish Encyclopedia. New York: Funk and Wagnalls, 1906. 12 vols.

Although in some respects this work is out of date today, it contains important historical data.

United Synagogue of America
National Academy for Adult Jewish Studies. *Catalogue Eternal Light Films.* New York, 1969

This catalogue lists the kinescopes of the Eternal Light film series produced by the Jewish Theological Seminary of America with NBC. The films deal with Jewish life in America, and portray the family life and experiences of varied individuals.

Appendixes

1
Jewish life in fiction

Adler, Marjorie D.
A Sign Upon My Hand. Garden City, New York: Doubleday, 1964
Agnon, Samuel J.
The Bridal Canopy (Galicia). New York: Schocken Books, 1967
Agnon, Samuel J.
Two Tales (Israel). New York: Schocken Books, 1966
Aleichem, Sholom
Adventures of Mottel, The Cantor's Son (short stories). London: Collier, 1961·
Aleichem, Sholom
The Old Country (short stories). New York: Crown, 1964
Alpert, Hollis
The Claimant (post-war Germany). New York: Dial Press, 1968
Angoff, Charles
Between Day and Dark (Boston, U.S.A.). New York: Barnes, 1957
Angoff, Charles
The Bitter Spring (New York, U.S.A.). New York: Yoseloff, 1961
Angoff, Charles
Summer Storm (New York, U.S.A.). New York: Yoseloff, 1963
Arnold, Elliott
A Night of Watching (Denmark). New York: Scribner, 1967
Asch, Sholom
East River (New York, U.S.A.). New York: Putnam, 1946
Asch, Sholom
The Nazarene (historical). London: Routledge, 1939
Ayalti, Hanan
No Escape from Brooklyn (U.S.A.). New York: Twayne, 1966

Barker, Shirley
Strange Wives (Rhode Island, 17th Century). New York: Crown, 1963
Baron, Alexander
The Lowlife (London, England). New York: Barnes, 1964
Bellow, Saul
Herzog (U.S.A.). New York: Viking, 1964
Bellow, Saul
Mr. Sammler's Planet (U.S.A.). New York: Viking, 1970
Benaya, Margaret
The Levelling Wind (Israel). New York: Pantheon, 1958
Berger, Zdena
Tell Me Another Morning (Czechoslovakia). New York: Harper, 1961
Bermant, C. I.
Ben Preserve Us (Scotland). New York: Holt, Rinehart and Winston, 1966
Bermant, C. I.
Berl Make Tea (England). New York: Holt, Rinehart and Winston, 1966
Bermant, C. I.
Jericho Sleep Alone (Scotland). New York: Holt, Rinehart and Winston, 1966
Blocker, Joel
Israeli Stories (short stories). New York: Schocken, 1962
Buller, H.
One Man Alone (Montreal). Toronto: National Book Club, 1963
Caspary, Vera
A Chosen Sparrow (Austria). New York: Putnam, 1964
Charles, Gerda
The Crossing Point (England). New York: Knopf, 1961
Charles, Gerda
A Slanting Light (England). New York: Knopf, 1961
Charyn, Jerome
Once upon a Droshky (New York, U.S.A.). New York: McGraw-Hill, 1964
Condon, Richard
An Infinity of Mirrors (Germany and France). New York: Random, 1964
Dayan, Yael
Death Had Two Sons (Israel). New York: Dell, 1968
Elman, Richard
The 28th Day of Elul (Israel and Hungary). New York: Scribner, 1967
Epstein, Seymour
Leah (New York, U.S.A.). Boston: Little, Brown, 1964
Epstein, Seymour
The Successor (New York, U.S.A.). New York: Scribner, 1961
Ettingen, Elzbieta
Kindergarten (Holocaust). New York: Houghton Mifflin, 1970

Fast, Howard
Agrippa's Daughter (historical). Garden City, New York: Doubleday, 1964
Field, Hermann
Angry Harvest (Poland). New York: Apollo, 1958
Fielding, Gabriel
The Birthday King (Germany). New York: Morrow, 1963
Fineman, Morton
Christmas Is Everywhere Including Asia Minor (U.S.A.). New York: Norton, 1966
Fruchter, Norman
Coat upon a Stick (New York, U.S.A.). New York: Simon and Schuster, 1963
Fuchs, Daniel
Three Novels (New York, U.S.A.). New York: Basic Books, 1961
Fuks, Ladislav
Mr. Theodore Mundstock (Czechoslovakia). New York: Grossman, 1968
Glanville, Brian
The Bankrupts (London, England). London: Cape, 1958
Glanville, Brian
Diamond (England). New York: Farrar, Straus and Giroux, 1962
Gold, Herbert
Fathers (Cleveland, U.S.A.). New York: Random, 1967
Gold, Herbert
Love and Like (short stories). New York: Dial, 1960
Gordon, Noah
The Rabbi (U.S.A.). New York: McGraw-Hill, 1965
Gourse, R. Leslie
With Gall and Honey (Israel). New York: Avon, 1962
Graham, Gwethalyn
Earth and High Heaven (Montreal). Philadelphia: Lippincott, 1944
Green, G.
The Last Angry Man (New York, U.S.A.). New York: Scribner, 1965
Greenberg, Joanne
The King's Person (England, 12th Century). New York: Holt, Rinehart and Winston, 1963
Habe, Hans
The Mission (Austria). New York: Coward-McCann, 1966
Hartog, Jan de
The Inspector (Europe and North Africa). New York: Atheneum, 1960
Hempstone, Smith
In the Midst of Lions (Israel). New York: Harper and Row, 1968
Herrick, William
The Itinerant (U.S.A. and Spain). New York: McGraw-Hill, 1967

Hersey, John
The Wall (Poland). New York: Knopf, 1950
Hesky, Olga
The Serpent's Smile (Israel). New York: Dodd, Mead, 1967
Hesky, Olga
Time for Treason (Israel). New York: Dodd, Mead, 1967
Hilsenrath, Edgar
Night (Ukraine). New York: Doubleday, 1948
Hobson, Laura Z.
Gentleman's Agreement (New York, U.S.A.). New York: Avon, 1968
Horowitz, G.
Home Is Where You Start From (New York, U.S.A.). New York: Norton, 1968
Howe, Irving
A Treasury of Yiddish Stories (short stories). New York: World, 1968
Hubler, Richard G.
The Soldier and the Sage (historical). New York: Crown, 1966
Ikor, Roger
The Sons of Avrom (France). New York: Putnam, 1958
Israel, Charles E.
Rizpah (historical). New York: Simon and Schuster, 1961
Jacobson, Dan
The Beginners (South Africa, Israel, and England). New York: Macmillan, 1966
Jacobson, Dan
The Zulu and the Zeide (short stories). New York: Macmillan, 1966
Jerome, Victor J.
The Paper Bridge (London, England). New York: Citadel, 1966
Jessey, Cornelia
The Plough and the Harrow (U.S.A.). New York: Sheed, 1961
Kahn, Sholom
A Whole Loaf (short stories). New York: Vanguard, 1962
Kasdan, Sara
So It Was Just a Simple Wedding (U.S.A.). New York: Vanguard, 1961
Kaufmann, Myron S.
Remember Me to God (U.S.A.). Philadelphia: Lippincott, 1957
Kavinoky, Bernice
Honey from a Dark Hive (U.S.A.). New York: Popular Library, 1956
Kemelman, Harry
Friday the Rabbi Slept Late (U.S.A.). New York: Crown, 1964
Kemelman, Harry
Saturday the Rabbi Went Hungry (U.S.A.). New York: Crown, 1966
Klein, Abraham M.
The Second Scroll (Montreal, Europe, and Israel). New York: Knopf, 1951

Klein-Haparash, Jacob
He Who Flees the Lion (Rumania). New York: Atheneum, 1963
Kreisel, Henry
The Rich Man (Toronto and Austria). Toronto: McClelland and Stewart, 1948
Langfus, Anne
The Whole Land Brimstone (Poland). New York: Pantheon Books, 1962
Lauer, Stefanie
Home is the Place (Germany). New York: Knopf, 1957
Leftwich, Joseph
Yisroel (short stories). New York: Yoseloff, 1963
Levin, Meyer
Eva (Germany). New York: Pocket Books, 1960
Levin, Meyer
The Fanatic (U.S.A. and Europe). New York: Simon and Schuster, 1964
Levin, Meyer
The Old Bunch (U.S.A. and Chicago). New York: McFadden, 1962
Lewis, Robert
Michel, Michel (France). New York: Simon and Schuster, 1967
Malamud, Bernard
The Assistant (New York, U.S.A.). New York: Farrar, Straus and Giroux, 1957
Malamud, Bernard
The Fixer (Russia). New York: Farrar, Straus and Giroux, 1966
Malamud, Bernard
Idiots First (short stories). New York: Farrar, Straus and Giroux, 1963
Malamud, Bernard
The Magic Barrel (short stories). New York: Farrar, Straus and Giroux, 1958
Mankowitz, Wolf
A Kid for Two Farthings (England). New York: Deutsch, 1953
Mankowitz, Wolf
The Mendelman Fire (short stories). Boston: Little, Brown, 1957
Mann, Thomas
Joseph and His Brothers (historical). New York: Knopf, 1948
Markfield, Wallace
To an Early Grave (New York, U.S.A.). New York: Simon and Schuster, 1964
Memmi, Albert
The Pillar of Salt (Tunisia). New York: Grossman, 1963
Memmi, Albert
Strangers (Tunisia). New York: Grossman, 1959
Neshamit, Sarah
The Children of Mapu Street (Holocaust). Philadelphia: Jewish Publication Society, 1970

Moll, Elick
Memoir of Spring (New York, U.S.A.). New York: Putnam, 1961
Moll, Elick
Seidman and Son (New York, U.S.A.). New York: Signet, 1960
Newman, C. J.
We Always Take Care of Our Own (Montreal). Toronto: McClelland and Stewart, 1965
Osterman, Marjorie K.
Damned If You Do – Damned If You Don't (U.S.A.). New York: Avon, 1963
Peretz, Isaac L.
In This World and the Next (short stories). New York: Avon, 1958
Popkin, Chaim
The Chosen (Brooklyn, U.S.A.). New York: Ronald, 1967
Popkin, Zelda
Herman Had Two Daughters (U.S.A., post-World-War-I). Toronto: McClelland and Stewart, 1968
Rawicz, Piot
Blood from the Sky (Europe). New York: Harcourt, Brace and World, 1964
Ribalow, Harold U.
A Treasury of American Jewish Stories (short stories). New York: Yoseloff, 1958
Richler, Mordecai
The Apprenticeship of Duddy Kravitz (Montreal). London: Deutsch, 1959
Richler, Mordecai
Son of a Smaller Hero (Montreal). Toronto: McClelland and Stewart, 1965
Rossner, Judith
To the Precipice (New York, U.S.A.). New York: Morrow, 1966
Rosten, Leo C.
The Education of Hyman Kaplan (New York, U.S.A.). New York: Harcourt, Brace, 1944
Rosten, Leo C.
The Return of Hyman Kaplan (New York, U.S.A.). New York: Harper, 1959
Roth, Henry
Call It Sleep (New York, U.S.A.). New York: Avon, 1964
Roth, Philip
Goodbye Columbus (short stories). New York: Bantam, 1963
Roth, Philip
Letting Go (U.S.A.). New York: Random, 1962
Roth, Philip
Portnoy's Complaint (U.S.A.). New York: Random, 1969
Rothberg, Abraham
The Heir of Cain (Switzerland). New York: Putnam, 1966

Rothchild, Sylvia
Sunshine and Salt (U.S.A.). New York: Simon and Schuster, 1964
St. John, Robert
The Man Who Played God (Hungary and Poland). Garden City, New York: Doubleday, 1963
Salaman, Esther
The Fertile Plain (Russia). New York: Abelard, 1957
Samuel, Edwin
A Coat of Many Colors (short stories). New York: Abelard, 1960
Samuel, Edwin
My Friend Musa (short stories). New York: Abelard, 1963
Schechtman, Elya
Erev (Russia). New York: Crown, 1967
Schoonover, Lawrence
Key of Gold (historical). Boston: Little, Brown, 1968
Schulberg, Budd W.
What Makes Sammy Run (U.S.A.). New York: Bantam, 1961
Schulz, Bruno
The Street of Crocodiles (Poland). New York: Walker, 1963
Schwarz-Bart, Andre
The Last of the Just (Europe). New York: Bantam Books, 1961
Shamir, Moshe
David's Stranger (historical). New York: Abelard, 1965
Silberstang, Edwin
Nightmare of the Dark (Austria, Germany, and Switzerland). New York: Knopf, 1967
Simon, Joan
Portrait of a Father (New York, U.S.A.). New York: Atheneum, 1960
Simon, Solomon
In the Thicket (Russia). Philadelphia: Jewish Publications Society, 1963
Simonhoff, Harry
The Chosen One (Europe, 16th Century). New York: Barnes, 1964
Sinclair, Jo
Anna Teller (Hungary and U.S.A.). New York: McKay, 1960
Singer, Isaac B.
The Family Moskat (Poland). New York: Farrar, Straus and Giroux, 1965
Singer, Isaac B.
Gimpel the Fool (short stories). New York: Farrar, Straus and Giroux, 1957
Singer, Isaac B.
The Magician of Lublin (Poland, 19th Century). New York: Farrar Straus and Giroux, 1960

Rothberg, Abraham
The Song of David Freed (U.S.A.). New York: Putnam, 1968
Singer, Isaac B.
The Manor (Poland). New York: Farrar, Straus and Giroux, 1967
Singer, Isaac B.
Satan in Goray (Poland, 17th Century). New York: Farrar, Straus and Giroux, 1955
Singer, Isaac B.
Short Friday (short stories). New York: Farrar, Straus and Giroux, 1964
Singer, Isaac B.
The Slave (Poland, 17th Century). New York: Farrar, Straus and Giroux, 1968
Singer, Isaac B.
The Spinoza of Market Street (short stories). New York: Farrar, Straus and Giroux, 1961
Singer, Isaac J.
The Brothers Ashkenazi (Poland, 19th Century). New York: Knopf, 1936
Solomon, Ruth F.
The Candlesticks and the Cross (Russia). New York: Putnam, 1967
Stampfer, Judah L.
Sol Myers (New York, U.S.A.). New York: Macmillan, 1962
Stein, David L.
Scratch One Dreamer (Toronto). Indianapolis: Bobbs-Merrill, 1967
Stern, Daniel
Who Shall Live, Who Shall Die (New York, U.S.A.). New York: Crown, 1963
Sulkin, Sidney
The Family Man (Boston, U.S.A.). New York: McKay, 1962
Tarr, Herbert
The Conversion of Chaplain Cohen (U.S.A.). New York: Geis, 1963
Tarr, Herbert
Heaven Help Us (U.S.A.). New York: Random, 1968
Uris, Leon
Exodus (Europe and Israel). Garden City, New York: Doubleday, 1958
Uris, Leon
Mila 18 (Poland). Garden City, New York: Doubleday, 1961
Viertel, Joseph
The Last Temptation (Europe and Israel). New York: Simon and Schuster, 1955
Wallant, Edward L.
The Human Season (U.S.A.). New York: Harcourt, Brace, 1960
Wallant, Edward L.
The Pawnbroker (New York, U.S.A.). New York: Harcourt, Brace, 1961

Wallant, Edward L.
The Tenants of Moonbloom (New York, U.S.A.). New York: Harcourt, Brace, 1963
Weidman, Jerome
The Enemy Camp (U.S.A.). New York: Random, 1958
Weidman, Jerome
I Can Get It for You Wholesale (New York, U.S.A.). New York: Random, 1962
Weidman, Jerome
The Sound of Bow Bells (U.S.A.). New York: Random, 1962
West, M.
Tower of Babel (Middle East). New York: Morrow, 1968
Wiesel, Elie
The Accident (U.S.A. and Europe). New York: Hill and Wang, 1962
Wiesel, Elie
Dawn (Palestine). New York: Hill and Wang, 1961
Wiesel, Elie
The Gates of the Forest (U.S.A. and Europe). New York: Holt, Rinehart and Winston, 1966
Wiesel, Elie
The Town Beyond the Wall (France and Hungary). New York: Atheneum, 1964
Wiesel, Elie
A Beggar in Jerusalem (Israel). New York: Macmillan, 1970
Wilchek, Stella
Ararat (South America and Austria). New York: Harper, 1962
Wilson, S. J.
Hurray for Me (New York, U.S.A.). New York: Crown, 1964
Wiseman, Adele
The Sacrifice (Winnipeg, Canada). Toronto: Macmillan, 1958
Wouk, Herman
The City Boy (New York, U.S.A.). New York: Doubleday, 1952
Wouk, Herman
Marjorie Morningstar (New York, U.S.A.). New York: Doubleday, 1955
Yaffe, James
Mister Margolies (New York, U.S.A.). New York: Random, 1962
Yaffe, James
Nobody Does You Any Favors (New York, U.S.A.). New York: Putnam, 1966
Zador, Henry
Hear the Word (historical). New York: McGraw-Hill, 1962
Zangwill, Israel
The King of Schnorrers (short stories). New York: Yoseloff, 1960
Zevin, Israel
The Marriage Broker (short stories). New York: Putnam, 1960

2
World Jewish population

The following statistics are reprinted by permission of *American Jewish Year Book, 1969,* published by The American Jewish Committee and The Jewish Publication Society of America.

TABLE 1
Estimated Jewish population in Europe, 1968

Country	Total population[a]	Jewish population
Albania	1,965,000	300
Austria	7,323,000	12,500
Belgium	9,581,000	40,500
Bulgaria	8,310,000	7,000
Czechoslovakia	14,305,000	15,000
Denmark	4,839,000	6,000
Finland	4,664,000	1,700
France	49,866,000	535,000
Germany	76,000,000	30,000[b]
Gibraltar	25,000	650
Great Britain	55,068,000	410,000
Greece	8,716,000	6,500
Hungary	10,217,000	80,000
Ireland	2,899,000	5,400
Italy	52,354,000	35,000
Luxembourg	335,000	1,000
Malta	319,000	50
Netherlands	12,743,000	30,000
Norway	3,785,000	750
Poland	32,207,000	21,000
Portugal	9,505,000	650
Rumania	19,285,000	100,000
Spain	32,140,000	7,000
Sweden	7,908,000	13,000
Switzerland	6,071,000	20,000
Turkey	32,710,000	39,000[c]
USSR	237,914,000	2,594,000[c]
Yugoslavia	20,186,000	7,000
TOTAL	721,240,000	4,019,000

a United Nations, Statistical Office, *Monthly Bulletin of Statistics,* and other sources, including local publications.
b Includes East Germany, about 1,300.
c Includes Asian regions of the USSR and Turkey.

TABLE 2
Estimated Jewish population in North, Central and South America, and the West Indies, 1968

Country	Total population[a]	Jewish population
Canada	20,772,000	280,000
Mexico	47,267,000	30,000
United States	201,166,000	5,870,000
TOTAL NORTH AMERICA	269,205,000	6,180,000
Barbados	249,000	100
Costa Rica	1,594,000	1,500
Cuba	7,937,000	1,700
Curacao	148,000	700
Dominican Republic	3,889,000	350
El Salvador	3,267,000	300
Guatemala	4,864,000	1,500
Haiti	4,674,000	150
Honduras	2,535,000	150
Jamaica	1,913,000	600
Nicaragua	1,848,000	200
Panama	1,372,000	2,000
Trinidad	1,010,000	300
TOTAL CENTRAL AMERICA AND WEST INDIES	35,300,000	9,550
Argentina	23,617,000	500,000
Bolivia	3,852,000	4,000
Brazil	88,209,000	140,000
Chile	9,351,000	35,000
Colombia	19,191,000	10,000
Ecuador	5,695,000	2,000
Paraguay	2,231,000	1,200
Peru	12,772,000	4,000
Surinam	363,000	500
Uruguay	2,818,000	54,000
Venezuela	9,686,000	12,000
TOTAL SOUTH AMERICA	177,785,000	762,700
TOTAL	482,290,000	6,952,250

a See Table 1, note a.

TABLE 3

Estimated Jewish population in Asia, 1968

Country	Total population[a]	Jewish population
Afghanistan	16,113,000	800
Burma	25,811,000	200
China	720,000,000	20
Cyprus	622,000	30
Hong Kong	3,927,000	200
India	523,893,000	15,000
Indonesia	112,825,000	100
Iran	26,284,000	80,000
Iraq	8,440,000	2,500
Israel	2,841,000[b]	2,436,000
Japan	101,090,000	1,000
Lebanon	2,520,000	3,000
Pakistan	109,520,000	250
Philippines	35,933,000	500
Singapore	1,988,000	600
Syria	5,570,000	4,000
TOTAL	1,697,377,000	2,544,200

a See Table 1, note a.

b This total excludes population under Israeli control at the end of the 1967 war.

TABLE 4

Estimated Jewish population in Australia and New Zealand, 1968

Country	Total population[a]	Jewish population
Australia	12,031,000	69,500[b]
New Zealand	2,751,000	5,000
TOTAL	14,782,000	74,500

a See Table 1, note a.

b According to an interim report on 1966 census (*Jewish Chronicle*, London, December 29, 1967).

TABLE 5
Estimated Jewish population in Africa, 1968

Country	Total population[a]	Jewish population
Algeria	12,943,000	1,500
Congo Republic	16,730,000	300
Egypt	30,907,000	1,000
Ethiopia	23,667,000	12,000
Kenya	10,209,000	700
Libya	1,802,000	100
Morocco	14,580,000	50,000
Republic of South Africa	18,733,000	114,800
Rhodesia	4,530,000	5,000
Tunisia	4,560,000	10,000
Zambia (Northern Rhodesia)	3,945,000	800
TOTAL	142,606,000	196,200

a See Table 1, note a.

3

State of Israel, distribution of population by habitation and age group

Source: *Facts about Israel, 1970* (Jerusalem, Information Division, Ministry of Foreign Affairs, 1970), pp. 56-57.

Population, 1 January 1969, by type of habitation

Type of town, village, etc.	Population (thousands)	Per-cent	Local-ities
JEWS			
Towns	1,734.4	71.2	25
Urban areas	425.2	17.4	48
Total Urban	2,159.6	88.6	73
Large villages	21.6	0.9	7
Small villages	28.1	1.2	53
Moshavim	122.1	5.0	344
Collective moshavim	5.0	0.2	22
Kibbutzim	84.1	3.5	235
Institutions, farms, etc.	12.1	0.5	45
Living outside villages	2.2	0.1	–
Total Rural	275.2	11.4	706
JEWS: TOTAL	2,438.8	100.0	779
NON-JEWS			
Towns	150.5	37.1	8
Urban areas	24.7	6.1	3
Total Urban	175.2	43.2	11
Large villages	145.4	35.8	39
Small villages	48.0	11.8	59
Moshavim and kibbutzim	0.6	0.1	–
Beduin tribes	35.2	8.7	(45)
Institutions, farms, etc.	0.1	0.0	1
Living outside villages	1.7	0.4	–
Total Rural	231.0	56.8	99
NON-JEWS TOTAL	406.2	100.0	110
COMPLETE POPULATION			
Towns	1,884.9	66.4	27
Urban areas	449.9	15.8	50
Total Urban	2,334.8	56.8	99
Large villages	167.0	5.9	46
Small villages	76.1	2.7	112
Moshavim	122.5	4.3	344
Collective moshavim	5.1	0.2	22
Kibbutzim	84.2	3.0	235
Beduin tribes	35.2	1.2	(45)
Institutions, farms, etc.	18.2	0.4	46
Living outside villages	3.9	0.1	–
Total Rural	506.3	17.8	805
COMPLETE POPULATION: TOTAL	2,841.1	100.0	882

Distribution of population, 1 January 1969,
by age-groups

AGE	PERCENTAGES					
	Jews	Moslems	Christians	Druzes	Non-Jews	Total
0 - 14	30.6	52.6	38.1	48.9	49.7	33.4
15 - 29	25.8	23.5	25.2	23.8	23.9	25.5
30 - 44	17.0	12.6	17.8	13.6	13.6	16.4
45 - 64	19.8	7.6	12.9	9.3	8.6	18.2
65 and over	6.8	3.7	6.0	4.4	4.2	6.5

4

Addresses of publishers

Aldine Publishing
320 W. Adams Street
Chicago, Illinois 60606

American Jewish Yearbook
165 E. 56th Street
New York, N.Y. 10022

American Journal of Orthopsychiatry
1700 Eighteenth Street N.W.
Washington, D.C., 20009

American Journal of Sociology
University of Chicago Press
Chicago, Illinois 60637

Anti-Defamation League of B'nai B'rith
315 Lexington Avenue
New York, N.Y. 10016

Asian and African Studies
Israel Oriental Society
Hebrew University
Jerusalem, Israel

Association Press
291 Broadway
New York, N.Y. 10007

B'nai B'rith Hillel Foundation
1640 Rhode Island Avenue N.W.
Washington, D.C. 20036

B'nai B'rith Youth Organization
1640 Rhode Island Avenue N.W.
Washington, D.C. 20036

Burning Bush Press
218 E. 70th Street
New York, N.Y. 10021

Canadian Jewish Congress
493 Sherbrooke Street W.
Montreal, Quebec

C.C.A.R. Journal
(Central Conference
of American Rabbis)
790 Madison Avenue
New York, N.Y. 10021

Center for Urban Education
33 W. 42nd Street
New York, 10036

Child Welfare League of America
44 E. 23rd Street
New York, N.Y. 10010

Cleveland College of Jewish Studies
2030 S. Taylor Road
Cleveland, Ohio 44118

Commentary
165 E. 56th Street
New York, N.Y. 10022

Congress Bi-Weekly
(American Jewish Congress)
15 E. 84th Street
New York, N.Y. 10028

Conservative Judaism
3080 Broadway
New York, N.Y. 10027

Council of Jewish Federations
and Welfare Funds
315 Park Avenue S.
New York, N.Y. 10010

Council Woman
National Council of Jewish Women
1 W. 47th Street
New York, N.Y. 10036

Dimensions in American Judaism
Union of American
Hebrew Congregations
838 Fifth Avenue
New York, N.Y. 10021

Dispersion and Unity
Jewish Agency
515 Park Avenue
New York, N.Y. 10022

Edutext Publications
82 Fryent Way
London, N.S. 9
England

Etgar
Zionist Organization of Canada
188 Marlee Avenue
Toronto 19, Ontario

The Family Coordinator
National Council on Family Relations
1219 University Avenue S.E.
Minneapolis, Minnesota 55414

Federation of Jewish Philanthropies
130 E. 59th Street
New York, N.Y. 10022

Philipp Feldheim Inc. Publications
381 Grand Street
New York 2, N.Y.

Hadassah Magazine
Hadassah Women's Zionist
Organization
65 E. 52nd Street
New York, N.Y. 10022

The Harvill Press
23 Lower Belgrave Street
London, S.W.1, England

Hawthorn Books
70 Fifth Avenue
New York, N.Y. 10011

Herzl Press
515 Park Avenue
New York, N.Y. 10022

Human Relations
Tavistock Institute
of Human Relations
Plenum Press, Donington House
30 Norfolk Street
W.C.2 London, England

Israel Digest
P.O. Box 92
Jerusalem, Israel

Israel Horizons
Suite 700
150 Fifth Avenue
New York, N.Y. 10011

The Israel Institute
of Applied Social Research
14 George Washington Street
P.O. Box 7150
Jerusalem, Israel

Israel Magazine
Israel Publishing Company
11401 Roosevelt Boulevard
Philadelphia, Pennsylvania 19154

Jewish Agency
515 Park Avenue
New York, N.Y. 10022

Jewish Book Annual
15 E. 26th Street
New York, N.Y. 10010
(Jewish Book Council of America)

Jewish Heritage
1640 Rhode Island Avenue N.W.
Washington, D.C. 20031

The Jewish Journal of Sociology
55 New Cavendish Street
London W.1, England

Jewish Publication Society
of America
222 N. 15th Street
Philadelphia, Pennsylvania 19102

The Jewish Social Service Quarterly
(Now Journal of Jewish Communal
Service)

Jewish Social Studies
521 W. 122nd Street, Room 33
New York, N.Y. 10027
(Conference on Jewish Social Studies)

The Jewish Social Work Forum
Alumni Association
Wurzweiler School of Social Work
Yeshiva University
55 Fifth Avenue
New York, N.Y. 10003

Jewish Standard
44 Wellington Street E.
Toronto 1, Ontario

Jossey Bass Publishers
615 Montgomery Street
San Francisco, California 94111

Journal of Jewish Communal Service
National Conference of Jewish
Communal Service
31 Union Square
New York, N.Y. 10003

Journal of Marriage and the Family
National Council on Family Relations
1219 University Avenue S.E.
Minneapolis, Minnesota 55414

Judaism
15 E. 84th Street
New York, N.Y. 10028

Leo Baeck Institute
129 E. 73rd Street
New York, N.Y. 10021

Midstream
Theodor Herzl Foundation
515 Park Avenue
New York, N.Y. 10022

Milbank Memorial Fund Quarterly
Milbank Memorial Fund
40 Wall Street
New York, N.Y. 10005

National Council of Jewish Women
1 W. 47th Street
New York, N.Y. 10036

National Jewish Monthly
1640 Rhode Island Avenue, N.W.
Washington, D.C. 20036
(B'nai B'rith)

National Jewish Welfare Board
15 E. 26th Street
New York, N.Y. 10010

Orah Magazine
1500 St. Catherines Street W.
Suite 318
Montreal 107, Quebec

Permagon Press
Maxwell House, Fairview Park
Elmsford, N.Y. 10523

The Press of Case Western
Reserve University
Cleveland, Ohio 44106

Public Affairs Press
419 New Jersey Avenue, S.E.
Washington, D.C.

Rabbinical Council of America
84 Fifth Avenue
New York, N.Y. 10011

Reconstructionist
Jewish Reconstructionist Foundation
15 W. 86th Street
New York, N.Y. 10024

Response
Room 3C
160 W. 106th Street
New York, N.Y. 10025

Sabra Books
38 W. 32nd Street
New York, N.Y. 10001

Schocken Books
67 Park Avenue
New York, N.Y. 10016

Scripta Hierosolymitana
Hebrew University
Jerusalem, Magnes Press

Sexology
200 Park Avenue S.
New York, N.Y. 10003

Social Service Review
University of Chicago Press
5750 Ellis Avenue
Chicago, Illinois 60637

Social Science
Department of Sociology
University of Toledo
Toledo, Ohio 43601

Social Work
49 Sheridan Avenue
Albany, N.Y. 12210

Charles C. Thomas Publishers
301-327 E. Lawrence Avenue
Springfield, Illinois

Tradition
Rabbinical Council of America
84 Fifth Avenue
New York, N.Y. 10011

United Synagogue of America
3080 Braodway
New York, N.Y. 10027

United Synagogue of America
National Academy for Adult
Jewish Education
218 E. 70th Street
New York, N.Y. 10021

Viewpoints
Labor Zionist Movement of Canada
5780 Decelles Avenue
Suite 305
Montreal 26, Quebec

Thomas Yoseloff Publishers
11 E. 36th Street
New York, N.Y. 10016

Your Child
United Synagogue Commission
of Jewish Education
3080 Broadway
New York, N.Y. 10027

Valentine Mitchell
18 Cursitor Street
London, E.C.4, England

Yivo Institute for Jewish Research
1048 Fifth Avenue
New York, N.Y. 10028

Yivo Annual of Jewish Social Science
Yivo Institute for Jewish Research
1048 Fifth Avenue
New York, N.Y. 10028

Author index

Author index